REJOICE IN THY FESTIVAL

REJOICE
IN THY FESTIVAL

A TREASURY OF WISDOM, WIT
AND HUMOR FOR THE SABBATH
AND JEWISH HOLIDAYS · · ·

by PHILIP GOODMAN

BLOCH PUBLISHING COMPANY

NEW YORK   5716 - 1956

מוקדש
לאברהם, שרה ויהודית

CONTENTS

PREFACE

The stories presented in this collection reflect the spirit of the Jewish holy days and festivals, their historical background, manner of observance and significance.

These stories are both new and old. They are new to those who have never heard nor read them before. And even to those who already know them, they remain everlastingly new and fresh because they are beloved. The good ones, like old friends, are enjoyed over and over again. The question is: which are the good ones? They are all good! Much depends on the mood and taste of the reader. The selection of the stories presented here are, after all, but one person's judgment. Concerning this judgment, it might be apropos to repeat for the thousandth time the age-old warning on what to expect when you try to tell a story to a Jew. When you begin, he immediately cuts you short, saying: "First of all, I've already heard that story. As a matter of fact, I know a better version. What is more, I can tell it better."

Are there original stories? The answer generally must be given in the negative. However, different versions will be found, some attributed to different people and some given a new *Kvetch* or twist.

The sources, both written and oral, for Jewish wisdom, wit and humor are countless. The writer has heard many stories from the mouths of humorists, would-be comics and just ordinary folks. Among those who have done extraordinary work in recording Jewish folklore of a witty and humorous nature are Alter Druyanov, M. Lipson and Daniel Persky. Better known in this country are perhaps the books of Nathan Ausubel, S. Felix Mendelsohn and Jacob Richman. The bibliography includes only the more important works that were consulted. Many other sources were also examined. Some stories have been found in various versions in as many as fifteen different places. To give the original source for each story would be an unnecessary task, serving no particular purpose other than to reveal the humorless erudition of the writer. All the material has been adapted and rewritten by the author.

Acknowledgment is herewith made to the Jewish Publication Society of America for permission to reprint a number of stories from our *The Purim Anthology* (Philadelphia, 1949).

The illustrations are reproductions of woodcuts from the *Book of Customs* (Amsterdam, 1723).

My deep appreciation is due to Dr. Mortimer J. Cohen for the generosity of his judicious guidance. I am greatly indebted to Lionel Koppman for his many helpful and valuable suggestions. Solomon Feffer has graciously given me the benefit of his keen and sound criticism. The encouragement of Edward H. Bloch and Solomon Kerstein has made possible the publication of this book. The invaluable aid and infinite patience of my devoted wife Hanna have been a boon.

To readers who would know the spirit of the Jewish people as evinced in its sacred days we reiterate the command of the Bible: "And thou shalt rejoice in thy festival" (*Deuteronomy* 16.14).

New York, N.Y.   PHILIP GOODMAN
Hanukkah Eve, 5716

REJOICE IN THY FESTIVAL

Sanctifying the New Moon

Chapter One

REJOICE IN THY FESTIVAL

Deuteronomy 16.14

"A man's character may be determined by three things: by his pocketbook, by his cup (of drinking wine) and by his anger; and, some say, also by his laughter" (*Erubin* 65b).

The laughter of the Jews is in large measure a reflection of the stern history of the Jewish people. In the face of ever-recurring persecutions throughout the checkered centuries Jews have sought strength and comfort in their fervent faith and relief in their keen sense of humor. Release from emotional tension was most often found in laughter that often concealed their inner anxieties. The humor and, especially, the wit of the Jewish people are to a marked degree a barometer of their varied experiences. In the midst of their perennial tribulations the Jews developed the keen sense of wit that brought them inexhaustible fortitude to survive the destructive forces of oppression and injustice.

Indeed, the Jews are perhaps unique in that they have learned to convert their tears to laughter and have thus realized the words of Koheleth, "a time to weep

3

and a time to laugh" (*Ecclesiastes* 3.4). Humorous and witty stories teased the mind of the Jewish common man as an individual and gave him psychic relief from his anxieties, a sense of superiority over his enemies, and even a vicarious triumph over the anti-semites forever present in his unhappy experience (for example, "Combing One's Hair," page 39; "The Purim to Come," page 171; "A New Holiday," page 266). Inherent in such stories of wit and humor is not only the exhilaration of triumph over his foes but, what is more valuable and enduring, his dignity as a human being reasserted, a regained freedom and God's justice vindicated ("Behold, I am Poor," page 73; "A Harsh Decree," page 120; "The Priority of Judaism," page 229). For Jewish humor is frequently not merely mirth-provoking; it is also conducive to transmitting ethical values, and thus humanly elevating ("Sabbath Spice," page 30; "A Religious Disputation," page 181).

It is, therefore, not surprising that the butt of many of the stories created by Jews are the Jews themselves ("Stealing for the Sabbath Escorts," page 44; "Haman's Bribe," page 155). Perhaps the outstanding features of Jewish wit and humor are the irony and self-criticism that predominate. None is exempt from satire and ridicule—the pious *Hasid* and the "baptized" Jew, the rich and the poor, the ignoramus and the rabbi ("Truth and Falsehood," page 97; "Commandments for the Rich and the Poor," page 232). Jews poke fun at their enemies, neighbors and relatives, but especially at themselves. They can joke at their own short-comings, evidencing a remarkable capacity for self-criticism. Although much of Jewish humor is satirical, ridiculing ignorance, miserliness and hypocrisy, it does not necessarily arrogate to itself any conceit or false pride ("Room for One More," page 77; "The Lot of a Beautiful *Esrog,*" page 124).

Wit may be differentiated from humor by various interpretations. It has been said that wit originates in the mind while humor springs from the heart. Wit may be harsh and cruel or it may be penetrating and subtle ("Blessing the Sabbath Candles," page 19; "The Sabbath Honors Nearly All Guests," page 25). Humor is usually less critical and more tolerant ("A Sin in Tel Aviv," page 46; "The Right to Differ," page 56). Wit, according to Webster's dictionary, is often the "felicitous combination of words and thoughts by which unexpected resemblances between things apparently unlike are vividly set before the mind so as to produce a shock of pleasant surprise." Since much of specifically Jewish wit consists of puns or plays on words and requires an intimate knowledge of Jewish literature, particularly the Bible and Talmud in their original languages, it is difficult to convey a real understanding and appreciation of it in translation ("The Hands of Esau," page 51; "Penitential Prayers," page 70). Indeed, much of Jewish wit defies translation as the flavor of the original Hebrew or Yiddish is essential for true comprehension ("A Smart Son," page 81; *"Dayenu,"* page 204). We have therefore taken the liberty of editing and even completely rewriting some of the stories so that they might be intelligible to English readers.

Numerous stories dealing with varied aspects of Jewish life, both as to ideas and forms, can be considered pure Jewish wit ("Stealing on the Sabbath," page 42; "The *Shulhan Aruch* Devoured," page 215). Others may be adaptations of humorous stories of other peoples transferred into a Jewish setting. These, too, may be included in Jewish humor ("Wipe Off Your Lips," page 107; "A Prayer for Rain Is Answered," page 130). However, the adaptation of a story merely by changing the names of the characters to Jewish names or by the use of oddities of speech or pronunciation (the so-called Jewish dialect) cannot be interpreted as Jewish humor. Jewish wit and humor, mirroring the soul of the Jewish people, have a flavor all their own and may be distinguished from those of other peoples. They are usually rooted in Jewish ways of life. They frequently contain philosophical observations ("A Cantor Is Unheard," page 33; "A Greater Crime," page 98). They cut perhaps more sharply and deeply than that of other peoples. One fascinating facet of the Jewish witty story is that it frequently has a "pseudo-climax" and a "super-climax" ("Lights Out," page 41; "A Fifty-Fifty Proposition," page 98; "Conducting the *Seder*," page 207).

WIT AND HUMOR IN EVERY AGE

The treasury of Jewish literature, from ancient Bible, Talmud and medieval writings to modern Haskalah prose and articles, stories and books of today, contains a wealth of sparkling witticisms, clever puns and humorous anecdotes. Since the time when the *Book of Proverbs* was written until the modern period, proverbs, both clever and amusing, have given expression to Israel's response to life's experiences and its folk attitudes and wisdom ("Folk Proverbs," pages 63, 109, 129).

The Hasidic movement, founded by the Baal Shem Tov, induced in its adherents a sensitive religious spirit which emphasized mystical and joyful communion with God. The *Hasidim* worshipped God in a spirit of joy that was sought in all aspects of living ("Opening the Gates of Repentance," page 93; "A Simhas Torah Celebration," page 135). Indeed, the depressing gloom of their environment, the persecutions they suffered, and the daily hardship of life intensified their need for joy and happiness. Innumerable anecdotes grew up among the *Hasidim* expressive of this need and were recounted by their rabbis ("Unwarranted Humiliation," page 86; "A Negligible Duty," page 116; "A Rare Privilege," page 123; "A Public Fast Day Abolished," page 248).

Anecdotes—short stories usually based on single events that actually or purportedly involved famous Jewish personalities—are legion. These make their wise or witty points, not necessarily humorous, relative to Jewish customs and character. The stories and anecdotes told about rabbis and sages and sayings attributed to them, whether factual or fanciful, reveal by and large their true character—love for the Jewish people and their faith in God ("Apples for the Sabbath!" page 15; "A Bitter Feeling," page 17). Many of these same stories are attributed to more than one person. This uncertainty of origin does not in any way diminish their significance. Certain rabbis were especially renowned for their wit and humor. Anecdotes about their teachers were spread widely by the East European *Yeshivah* students in the nineteenth century; this may account for the recurring role of the rabbi in these tales. The stories of Levi Isaac of Berditchev and Israel Lipkin Salanter are truly legion ("The Jews Are a Wonderful People," page 53; "Repentant Jews," page 69; "Concern for Body and Soul," page 87; "The Missing Rabbi," page 90; "Supervising the *Matzah* Baking," page 186).

East European Jewry of the eighteenth century produced a number of famous humorists who have bequeathed to us a treasure-trove of wit and humor. Among those whose stories and sayings have been preserved are Motke Habad of Vilna ("Earning the Passover Supplies," page 187), Hershele Ostropoler, the beloved legendary character of Russia ("Hershele Faces a Dilemma," page 14; "Purim Wine," page 168), and Ephraim Greidiger of Galicia ("Extinguishing the Sabbath Candles," page 44). The town of Helm was the legendary town of many hair-raising and amusing incidents. Its "wise men" were the butt of many jokes and pranks ("Announcing the Sabbath in Helm," page 17; *"Selihos* in Helm," page 68; "A Festival Feud in Helm," page 136; "The Ten Commandments of Helm," page 239).

The Joy of Festivals

Holy days, festivals and fast days have provided the source of inspiration for a distinctively Jewish folklore literature. While much of it is based on astute interpretations of texts, the joyous character of these days served to develop among the plain folk and the scholarly a humorous literature.

The Talmud says that "Gladness means a festival" (*Megillah* 16b). This saying could be reversed in equal truth—"A festival means gladness." Indeed, Jewish festivals have always been occasions of beauty, good cheer and joy that brought color, rest and relaxation into the drab and burdensome life of Jews in all generations. On Sabbaths and festivals they threw off their work-a-day cares and sought renewal through both spiritual and physical joy. Unfortunately for some modern Jews, these joyous occasions have been permitted to degenerate into days of restriction and prohibition and thus boredom, for they fail to grasp their real intent.

The duty of rejoicing on holy days and festivals finds continuous expression throughout Jewish literature. In the Talmud and Codes of Law the spirit and manner of observing these days are thus prescribed:

"Rejoicing on a festival is a religious duty. Rabbi Eliezer said: 'A man has nothing else to do on a festival, only either to eat and drink or to sit and study.' Rabbi Joshua said: 'Divide it—half to eating and drinking and half to the House of Study . . . [In other words] half for the Lord and half for yourselves.' " (*Pesahim* 68b; *Betzah* 15b)

"A man is obligated to make his children and his household rejoice on a festival, as it is said: 'And thou shalt rejoice in thy feast and thou shalt be altogether joyful' (*Deuteronomy* 16.14–15). How does he make them rejoice? With wine. Rabbi Judah said: 'Men rejoice with what is suitable for them . . . namely, with wine. But with what do women rejoice?' Rabbi Joseph taught: 'In Babylonia women rejoice with many-colored garments and in *Eretz Israel* with ironed garments of linen.' " (*Pesahim* 109a)

"On festival days one should be joyous and in good spirits . . . In what manner should one rejoice . . . ? The little ones should be given toasted corn and almonds, the women dresses and jewels, according to one's means." (*Orach Hayyim,* Laws of Rejoicing on a Festival, 529.2)

The Midrash says: "God gave to the people of the world many holidays when they eat, drink and rejoice. They also go to theaters and circuses and as a result of their talk and behavior they irritate the Lord. The children of Israel do not behave thus. God gave them many holidays when they eat, drink and rejoice. They also go to synagogues and houses of study and give praise to the Lord." (*Yalkut Shimeoni,* Phinehas, 29)

Yehudah Halevi wrote: "Your penitence on fast days does not bring you nearer to God than your joy on Sabbaths and festivals if your joy is an outpouring of a sincere and devout heart . . . And if your joy rises up into song and dance, then it too becomes worship . . ." (*Sefer Ha-Kuzari,* II, 50)

Closer to our own times, the Lubavitsher Rabbi wisely said: "On the first day of each festival, God extends us an invitation to observe a day of rejoicing with Him; on the second day, we invite Him to rejoice with us. God commanded us to observe the first day of the festival; the second day we instituted ourselves." (*Siah Sarfei Kodesh* 5.70)

These lovely, delightful expressions concerning the observance of the Sabbath, festivals and even fast days are often found in the display of sharp wit and in recounting humorous tales.

THE HOLY SABBATH

Blessing the Lights

CHAPTER TWO

THE HOLY SABBATH

*T*HE joy of a day of rest, bringing relief and renewal of spirit after the humdrum routine and
soul-destroying drudgery of the weekdays, promised
blessed freedom and richer living to the Jew. "And
thou shalt call the Sabbath a delight," the princely
prophet proclaimed (Isaiah 58.13). The Sabbath itself
is an eternal memorial, commemorating the day that
God rested from His work of creation and the deliverance of the children of Israel from Egyptian bondage.
Our sages taught that the spiritual freedom and the in-
vigorating sense of life manifested in the Sabbath are
supreme joys; they transcend all the passing pleasures
of mundane living. Observance of the Sabbath brings
light, good cheer and joy in the Jewish home. "He who
enjoys the Sabbath will receive the desires of his heart"
(Shabbat 118b), the Talmud boldly declares. It is not
surprising, therefore, that the holy Sabbath and its
sacred traditions provide the occasion for numerous
witty stories and the subjects of frivolous ones.

Preparations for the Sabbath

"He who prepares on the eve of the Sabbath
will enjoy the Sabbath" (Abodah Zarah 3a) has

13

*been a guiding principle in Jewish life. Every
member of the family participates in getting
ready for the day of rest that is anxiously
awaited. The rabbis of old set an example by
doing manual labor in preparation for ushering in the Sabbath. The poor people skimped
throughout the week so that they could have
the necessities for observing the Sabbath properly. The urgency of Sabbath preparations,
which evoked the understanding sympathy of
Jewish sages, is delineated in some of the following stories.*

Hershele Faces a Dilemma

One Friday Hershele Ostropoler, the eighteenth century legendary character, visited Rabbi Baruch of Med-
ziboz.

"Why do you appear so downcast?" the rabbi asked.

"I am utterly confused and I need your advice,
rabbi."

"Ask and I will try to answer."

"Today I was given contradictory advice from two
sources and I am at a loss as to which one's advice to
follow," began Hershele, unfolding his tale of woe. "I
first met the Evil Spirit and I told him that I didn't
have the wherewithal to buy food for my family for
the Sabbath. What do you think he said? The Evil Spirit
advised me: 'Steal some silverware from Rabbi Baruch
and sell it. Then you'll be able to purchase your Sabbath needs.'

"Intending to pursue this practical advice, I started
towards your house. On the way I encountered the

Good Spirit who inquired as to my destination. Innocently, I revealed my intentions to him. In a threatening tone, he warned me: 'Hershele, you know that in the Torah it is written: Thou shalt not steal.'

"Now, Rabbi Baruch, I want to ask you. Shall I listen to the Evil Spirit and steal so that my family will be enabled to observe the Sabbath properly? Shall I obey the Good Spirit and permit my family to desecrate the holy day by not eating the prescribed three Sabbath meals?"

Rabbi Baruch understood the question and smiled. Instead of advice, he gave Hershele some money so that he would be able to meet the Sabbath needs of his family.

"Apples for the Sabbath!"

Rabbi Hayyim Halberstam of Sandz was in his study on a Friday afternoon making the necessary preparations to welcome Queen Sabbath. The quiet of the house was suddenly interrupted by the unannounced entrance of an old woman carrying a large basket of unappetizing apples. Rushing into the rabbi's study, the woman breathlessly began to pour forth her anguish.

"Rabbi, I am a poor peddler. I sell apples in the marketplace. Most of the day has already passed. I still haven't sold the fruit. And I don't have enough money to purchase food for the Sabbath."

The rabbi thought for a minute and then told the indigent woman to remain for a while in his house. Without wasting time, the rabbi donned his Sabbath clothes, placed the basket on his arm and hurried to the marketplace.

Standing in the main intersection, Rabbi Hayyim shouted:

"Apples for the Sabbath! Jews, buy apples for the Sabbath!"

A commotion immediately arose in the square as the Jews witnessed this strange sight. Their saintly rabbi was hawking apples—ordinary, green apples and even overripe ones! Nevertheless, everyone was most anxious to acquire the merit of reciting the blessing on fruit sanctified for the Sabbath by the rabbi. In no time at all, the rabbi sold the entire stock at a price above the market value.

The rabbi returned home and presented the earnings of his brief business venture to the woman.

"Here's your money for the apples," he said. "Hurry and prepare for the Sabbath."

PROVIDING FOR THE SABBATH

One Friday morning a rabbi, returning home from the services in the synagogue, met one of his congregants, known for his dire poverty, walking away from the house with what appeared to be a pair of large, silver candlesticks bulging from his coat. Sensing that he had discovered a thief, the rabbi nevertheless gently said to him:

"Don't be ashamed. I can understand that you don't have any money with which to purchase provisions for the Sabbath and that you brought your candlesticks as a pledge. Give me the candlesticks and I'll loan you two rubles."

A Bitter Feeling

On the eve of the Sabbath a poor, grief-stricken woman came to the sage Tzvi Lunshitzer with a chicken. Tearfully she explained that she could not find a gall in it and therefore feared that it was not kosher. What was she to do? The rabbi examined the chicken carefully and couldn't find the gall either. He tested it with his tongue to determine if it had the bitter taste of the gall but he couldn't taste any bitterness. Meanwhile the woman, with bated breath and an anxious look on her face, waited for the rabbi's decision.

Finally, the rabbi asked:

"Do you have any other meat for the Sabbath?"

"No, rabbi," the woman said sadly. "This chicken is the only food I have to feed my husband and four children."

"What can I do if I can't taste any bitterness," the rabbi said. "Here, you try. Perhaps you'll be able to taste it."

Unable to taste the gall, the woman cried in desperation:

"O, rabbi, how bitter it is! I taste only bitterness for my family will go hungry on the Sabbath . . ."

Hastily interrupting her, the sage declared:

"If you taste bitterness, it's *Kosher*. Take the chicken home and may you and yours enjoy the Sabbath."

Announcing the Sabbath in Helm

At the first snowfall of the winter, which occurred on the eve of a Sabbath, the wise people of Helm rejoiced. For the pure, white snow blanketed the streets of the town. But the joy of the townsfolk was shortlived as they realized that soon the beauty of the white carpet would be ruined when the sexton walked through the streets to announce the approach of the Sabbath.

This naturally presented a serious problem to the Helmites. The rabbi and the elders of the congregation were hastily summoned to an emergency meeting to grapple with this grave situation: how would it be possible for the sexton to fulfill his duty and yet not walk on the snow, lest he destroy its pure whiteness? The winter's day was short; time was of the essence. A decision had to be reached quickly. Ignoring the elders, the rabbi took matters in his own hands, and, in a reassuring voice, decreed:

"The duty of the sexton is clear. He must as usual announce the Sabbath but he shall not walk on the snow. Let the sexton be placed on a table and let him be borne through the streets of Helm by four elders of the congregation."

Friday Evening

The Sabbath is greeted with candle light, songs, wine and a festive meal. On Friday before sunset, the mother kindles the Sabbath candles, brightening the home. As the men-folk return from the synagogue, they sing Sholom Aleichem, a hymn of greeting to the Sabbath angels. Before the family sits down to enjoy the festive meal, the Sabbath is sanctified with the recital of the Kiddush over a cup of wine. These sacred traditions have been the object of numerous witticisms.

Blessing the Sabbath Candles

A certain rabbi's wife was well-known in the community as a shrew. She never hesitated to use her sharp tongue to heap abuses upon the head of her husband and to make his life miserable. While the mild-mannered rabbi bore his suffering in silence, the constant reproaches and nagging of his wife affected his ministry adversely. Determined to do something about it, the president of the congregation took it upon himself to visit the *Rebbetzin*.

"*Rebbetzin*," he said, "you know that the rabbi is beloved by all of us. He is, indeed, a shining light for the entire congregation. If you bless the Sabbath lights, why do you curse him?"

The shrew sharply retorted to the admonishing question:

"Mr. President, I promise you that if the rabbi will burn like the Sabbath lights, I'll bless him too!"

A Modern Innovation

A business woman was always scrupulous in fulfilling the commandment of lighting the Sabbath candles. One Friday she found to her consternation that she could not return home in time to kindle the lights. In desperation, she contrived an ingenious solution to the problem. She telephoned her home and instructed her maid to set the candles near the phone and to light them. When the maid had complied, the woman chanted the blessing for lighting the Sabbath candles into the mouthpiece of the telephone.

GREETING THE SABBATH ANGELS

The saintly Rabbi Israel Meir Ha-Kohen, better known as the author of *Hafetz Hayyim,* returned home from the synagogue on Friday evening with several guests. Omitting to sing *Sholom Aleichem,* he immediately recited the *Kiddush,* washed his hands, pronounced the benedictions for washing hands and for bread and sat down to eat.

The guests were amazed that the rabbi had failed to sing *Sholom Aleichem.* One of the guests hesitatingly asked the rabbi about this departure from Jewish custom.

The sage replied:

"The song *Sholom Aleichem* is a welcome to the ministering angels of the Sabbath. The angels don't require food while my guests whom I also want to welcome do need food. Therefore, I welcome my guests before the Sabbath angels."

WHEN ANGELS ARE NOT WELCOME

One man who had a well-earned reputation as a glutton was once asked:

"Why is it that on Friday evening just before the meal we greet the Sabbath angels and immediately bid them farewell—'Depart in peace'?"

It didn't take the glutton long to give an answer to the inquirer:

"Indeed, that's an excellent custom," he said. "It teaches you that at the time of a meal even an angel is superfluous."

Sanctifying the Sabbath with Wine

When Rabbi Jonathan Eibshitz of Prague was a child, his father gave him an empty flask and told him to go to the wine shop and get wine for *Kiddush* so that the Sabbath could be properly sanctified.

"Where's the money for the wine?" the child asked.

"With money anyone can get wine," the father replied.

Without saying anything more, Jonathan left.

In the evening when the family was gathered around the Sabbath table, the father, noticing the empty wine bottle, asked Jonathan:

"Where's the wine for *Kiddush?*"

"With wine anyone can recite *Kiddush*," Jonathan replied.

A Difficult Pupil

A farmer, concerned with the Jewish education of his ten-year-old son, arranged for a teacher to come to his home from a nearby city. Anxious to see rapid progress in his son's education, he made an offer to the teacher.

"As soon as my son can recite the Sabbath *Kiddush*," he said, "I'll give you a bonus in addition to your salary."

In a short time the teacher succeeded in imparting to his pupil a fairly good knowledge of the rudiments of the Hebrew language. However, when the educator tried to teach the boy to recite the *Kiddush*, he was unable to make any headway. He tried first one method, then another, all to no avail. Finally, he decided to experiment with a technique based upon the process of learning by association. Taking the boy outside, he walked with him to the house of Abraham, the nearest neighbor, and said to him:

"Let this house in which Abraham lives be a reminder to you of *Yom;* the next house of Isaac you should associate with *Ha-Shishi;* the next of Jacob will be *Va-Yechulu;* the following house of Joseph—*Ha-Shomayim.*"

In this manner—by having an association for each word of the *Kiddush*—the boy eventually succeeded in memorizing the entire prayer.

The teacher rightly felt that he had earned his bonus. He informed the farmer that his son was ready for the test.

On Friday evening the boy was given a goblet of wine. The family waited anxiously to hear how well he had learned his lesson, while the teacher, a guest at the table, was thinking how he would spend the bonus.

In a loud, clear voice, the boy began the *Kiddush:* "*Yom Ha-Shishi Ha-Shomayim . . .*"

The teacher angrily interrupted:

"Boy! Where's *Va-Yechulu?*"

Unabashed, the pupil replied:

"Teacher, *Va-Yechulu* is no more. He died yesterday."

KIDDUSH BY PROXY

A horse dealer was accustomed to recite the Friday evening *Kiddush* over a large cup of wine. As he said the *Kiddush,* he would bear in mind all the members of his household and thus release them from the obligation of reciting the sanctification over the wine.

During the meal, he sent his servant to feed the horses. Surprised that the servant returned very quickly, he inquired:

"Are you certain that you fed all the horses?"

"I gave the oldest horse a large sackful of hay," replied the servant, "and told him to bear in mind all the other horses."

The Reception of Guests

"The reception of guests is as important as the reception of the Sabbath," Rabbi Nahman of Bratzlav claimed. Moreover, the Talmud says that "the welcome of guests is more meritorious than the welcome of the Divine Presence" (Shabbat 127a). This generous attitude is especially evident on the Sabbath when householders anxiously seek poor persons to invite as table companions. Such hospitality frequently created strange situations and led to numerous humorous stories.

SABBATH HOSPITALITY

Jewish tradition prescribed that every householder should invite an itinerant beggar to his home for the Sabbath meals. One Friday night, a Jew invited a beggar whom he met in the synagogue. On the way home, he was surprised to notice that another beggar was following them. Turning to his invited guest, he asked him if he knew who the other beggar was.

The guest quietly replied:

"Oh, he's my son-in-law. When he married my daughter, I promised to support him. Therefore, wherever I eat, he also eats."

INDULGING IN SABBATH MEALS

A beggar arrived in town for the Sabbath. To his delight, he learned that there were two services in the synagogue on Saturday morning—an early one and a late one. Bright and early, the beggar appeared at the first service and at its conclusion he waited for the expected invitation to a Sabbath meal. The sexton duly extended to him an invitation to dine at his home. After the beggar had enjoyed a rather sumptuous meal, he politely excused himself and hurriedly returned to the synagogue where he waited until the late service was finished. The rabbi, who attended this *Minyan,* saw the stranger and asked him to join his family for the Sabbath. The beggar readily accepted the proffered hospitality and accompanied the rabbi to his home. Following *Kiddush,* the family seated itself around the festive Sabbath board. As they started to eat, the door opened and the sexton appeared on the threshold. He gaped in astonishment at the beggar who was about to start his second meal of the morning. The beggar unabashedly called to the sexton:

"Don't be ashamed. Come in and join us. You must be hungry, too!"

GUESTS FOR THE SABBATH

One Friday afternoon a small group of Jews arrived in a town and looked for a place to spend the Sabbath. Unable to find anyone willing to extend to them hospitality for the Sabbath, they finally went to the town's rabbi and told him of their predicament. When the rabbi learned of the ungraciousness of his townsmen, he quickly donned his Sabbath garments and told the visitors:

"Come with me to the next town. Perhaps the residents there will be more hospitable."

So saying, the rabbi led the group towards the outskirts of his town. As they were walking along, some of the surprised townsmen pursued the rabbi and the group of strangers and overtook them. They asked the rabbi the reason for his unexpected departure on the eve of the Sabbath.

"I won't remain here as long as there can't be found lodging and food for these visitors for the Sabbath," explained the rabbi. "I am going with them to the next town where we will undoubtedly be well-received."

The local townsmen learned their lesson and began competing among themselves for the honor of having the strangers as guests for the Sabbath.

The Sabbath Honors Nearly All Guests

A Lithuanian rabbi, who had a reputation for being a conceited and boastful person, was once a Sabbath guest of Rabbi Isaac Elhanan Spektor of Kovno. The latter, contrary to his real nature, was not overly hospitable. The Lithuanian, whose pride was severely hurt, asked his host why he was being treated differently than other rabbis who had been his guests.

Isaac Elhanan replied:

"We know that the Sabbath receives guests most warmly. For example, when the Day of Atonement

falls on a Sabbath, the latter yields its greatest pleasures
—eating and drinking. Why, therefore, doesn't the Sabbath permit the blowing of the *Shofar* when Rosh Hashanah coincides with it? The answer is really simple.
It is true that the Sabbath honors nearly all guests; however, it makes an exception with a guest who toots his
own horn."

AN UNWELCOME GUEST

A Hasid, on the way to his *Rebbe* with whom he intended to enjoy the Sabbath, met with an unfortunate
accident and had to observe the holy day in a little
town. He eventually reached the rabbi's home on Sunday afternoon. Weary in body and spirit, he explained
to the *Rebbe* the unforeseen circumstances that pre-
vented him from arriving in time for the Sabbath.

The rabbi reassured him:

"You know that when the holy days and festivals occur on a Sabbath they are welcomed with special prayers. Once when Tishah B'Av fell on a Sabbath, it complained to the Almighty, saying: 'Why should I be different from the other special days in the calendar? Why
is no provision made to welcome me on the Sabbath?'
To these questions, the Lord replied: 'A guest such as
you can come on a Sunday.' "

SHABBOS-KUGEL

A beggar appeared at the door of a wealthy but miserly Jew on a Sunday morning and pleaded for something to eat.

"Will you eat *Shabbos-Kugel?*" the rich man asked, invitingly.

"Why not?" the beggar said.

"Then come here next Saturday and I'll see if there'll be any left over."

SABBATH AT HOME

The rabbi of Apta was spending a Sabbath in the home of the preacher Yehiel Michel of Zlotzov. Despite the poverty of the preacher, he asked his wife to prepare special dishes that would satisfy his distinguished guest. He knew how much the rabbi enjoyed eating, especially the Sabbath meals.

Friday night when both men returned from the synagogue, the rabbi was astonished to observe the Sabbath candles set in potatoes, a towel in place of a cloth on the table and an ordinary drinking glass instead of a *Kiddush* cup.

Using no tact at all, the rabbi exclaimed:

"I'm amazed to see such poverty in your home!"

"God forbid!" denied the preacher. "I don't lack anything. My family has enough to eat and drink and we can even entertain guests."

"I am pleased to hear that," said the rabbi, unconvinced. "However, in my home I've beautiful linen tablecloths, a hand-wrought silver candelabrum and a golden cup for *Kiddush.*"

"How did you achieve such wealth?" innocently queried the preacher.

"I simply travel from town to town and teach Torah for which I'm well compensated."

"Why don't you use your beautiful possessions now to honor the Sabbath?" the preacher pressed further.

"As you see, I'm away from home, in exile, and I don't have my Sabbath objects with me."

Yehiel then retorted sharply:

"Your precious gold and silver is in your home and you're in exile; the reverse is true of me: I'm in my home with my beloved ones and guests and the silver and gold are in exile."

The Sabbath Meals

The joyous nature of the Sabbath is reflected in the festive meals with their table hymns (Zemiros) and special delicacies. The fresh, white, twisted loaf of bread (Hallah) and the stuffed (gefilte) fish are reserved for the enjoyment of the Sabbath. Of course, no Sabbath meal would be complete without the pudding (Kugel). Indeed, a Jewish proverb states: "A Sabbath without Kugel is like a bird without wings."

Expensive Hallah

A guest was enjoying a Sabbath meal at the home of a friend. Noticing that the guest was eating only the delicious *Hallah* but that he did not touch the plain bread, the host hinted delicately:

"Why don't you taste the bread?"

"Because *Hallah* is usually much better than plain bread," replied the guest.

"But you know that *Hallah* is more expensive."

"That doesn't matter," the guest said. "It's worth it!"

Fish in Honor of the Sabbath

Rabbi Samuel Shmelke Hurwitz of Nickolsburg was quite affluent and enjoyed a life of luxury while his brother Pinhas existed in dire poverty. One Sabbath Pinhas was invited to his brother's home. As befits a wealthy host, substantial portions of appetizing stuffed fish were served during the Friday evening meal.

"In my house we eat fish in honor of the Sabbath," remarked Pinhas.

His learned brother was amazed at this peculiar comment and asked:

"Isn't the Sabbath likewise honored in my house?"

Pinhas readily responded:

"What I mean is that in my home each member of the family receives only a small piece of fish, and even that's not the best, so that it's truly a real symbol of the honor we give to the Sabbath. Here I see that you eat fish for your own enjoyment."

The Priority of Kugel

A newly-wed couple came before a rabbi with the request that he issue a divorce to them. The rabbi asked them what led them to reach this grave decision after such a short married life.

The husband first presented his grievance:

"I work hard all week. When the Sabbath arrives, I feel I'm entitled to some slight enjoyment. Upon returning home from the morning services in the synagogue, I recite the *Kiddush*. My wife then serves stuffed fish, soup with noodles, chicken and vegetables, and when I cannot eat another morsel she brings out the *Kugel*. I demand that the *Kugel* be served first so that I can really enjoy eating it while I still have an appetite."

The young wife defended her action thus:

"It was a tradition in my father's house—which I feel binding upon me—that the *Kugel* is served at the end of the Sabbath meal. Rabbi, would you want me to violate a Jewish custom?"

The rabbi thoughtfully pondered for a while and then rendered his decision:

"Henceforth, two *Kugels* shall be served: one *Kugel* at the start of the Sabbath meal which will be eaten with appetite, and the second at the end, so that a Jewish custom won't be ignored. Now, return home and live in peace."

SABBATH SPICE

Emperor Hadrian once asked Rabbi Joshua ben Hananiah:

"What gives your Sabbath meat such a delightful aroma?"

"We have a spice called Sabbath which is cooked with the meat and this makes the pleasing aroma," the rabbi answered.

"Give me some of this seasoning!" the emperor ordered.

Joshua ben Hananiah replied:

"The spice is effective only for those who observe the Sabbath; however, it is of no value to those who do not honor the Sabbath."

Shabbat 119a

The Extra Soul for the Sabbath

While the congregants in the vestry room of the synagogue were enjoying the Third Meal of the Sabbath with words of Torah, songs and delicacies, the town *Apikorus* (heretic) entered and mockingly said:

"Eat and drink, Jews, for the *Neshamah Yeserah,* that Extra Soul that you possess today, requires nourishment."

"Why don't you join us?" Hershele Ostropoler cordially invited the non-believer. "You, too, have an Extra Soul."

"That's not so," indignantly exclaimed the *Apikorus.* "I've only one soul."

"That's what I mean," Hershele said. "Even that one is an extra soul for you."

In the Synagogue

The Sabbath in the synagogue is a day of prayer and teaching. The reading of the weekly portion of the Torah and the preaching of the rabbi or the Magid provide instruction. On the Sabbath, the cantor leads the congregation in prayer. The prominent role of the synagogue functionaries—Klei Kodesh (Holy Vessels)—in the Sabbath services made them topics for discussion.

A Preacher's Disillusionment

An itinerant preacher arrived in town on the eve of the Sabbath. The following morning he was invited to deliver the sermon in the synagogue. Using as his text the commandment "Honor the Sabbath day to keep it holy," the preacher spoke in eloquent tones and deeply-moving words of the severe punishment awaiting those who profane the day of rest, and called upon desecrators of the Sabbath to repent for their evil ways.

On Sunday morning the preacher made the rounds of the homes of the well-to-do congregants to claim his honorarium for preaching. Having been informed that Yoseph Mazik was a public violator of Jewish tradition who even had the effrontery to keep his shop open on the Sabbath, the preacher decided to pass his house by. Some force, however, drew him to the home of the Sabbath violator and, to his embarrassment and surprise, he was well received.

Without waiting to be asked, Mazik gave the preacher a handsome gift of money and praised him extravagantly for the sermon which he had heard so much about from others.

The preacher, thinking that his sermon had brought about a change of heart, quoted the following passage to Mazik:

"In the place where repentants stand, the completely righteous cannot remain."

"Oh, don't misunderstand me," the renegade said. "I haven't any intention of repenting. I hope, however, that as a result of your sermon, other storekeepers who are open on the Sabbath will repent. Then my store will be the only one open on Saturday and, at least for one day a week, I won't have any competition from these storekeepers."

A Cantor Is Unheard

Every Friday evening the *Hasidim* of Wolozin prayed with special warmth and fervent devotion. Swaying and chanting, they extended a royal welcome to Queen Sabbath.

Once a famous visiting cantor was invited to officiate at the services inaugurating the Sabbath. His rich, deep voice rang out loud and clear, drowning out the voices of the *Hasidim*.

In the middle of the night, the rabbi of the congregation had a dream in which a Sabbath angel appeared with the following complaint:

"The Sabbath angels are aggrieved that you didn't welcome them as you usually do every Sabbath with pious song."

Amazed at hearing this grievance, the rabbi, in an attempt to spare his *Hasidim* from reproof, explained:

"A guest cantor with a remarkably melodious voice conducted the services."

The angel then said:

"That's strange. The angels in heaven didn't hear anything!"

Attendance at Sabbath Services

At the annual membership meeting of a certain reform congregation, the rabbi delivered an impassioned plea urging the members to hold the only weekly service on Saturday morning instead of Sunday morning, as had been the practice. A member who never attended services threatened that he would resign from the congregation if the rabbi's proposal was approved. The rabbi asked the vociferous one why he was so violently opposed to the innovation.

Unhesitatingly, he replied:

"Rabbi, I just would rather not attend services on Sunday than not attend on the Sabbath."

PROMPT REMITTANCE

One Sabbath morning a stranger in the synagogue was invited to recite the blessings over the reading of the Torah. When his turn came, the sexton approached him and asked:

"How are you called?"

The stranger replied:

"Exchange 2–1234."

"No, no, no," the sexton said. "That's not what I meant. I mean, what is your name in Hebrew? What was your father's name?"

After getting the information, the sexton called the stranger to recite the blessings. He then gently hinted that it would be appropriate that the man pledge a contribution to the synagogue.

The stranger graciously responded:

"I'll give ten dollars."

He then removed his wallet from his pocket. Noticing the look of consternation on the sexton's face, he said, "But I always pay cash."

TAKING UP THE COLLECTION

The following anecdote is told of the late Rabbi Stephen S. Wise. When the offertory was being collected at a Friday evening service, he said to the congregants:

"Friends, tonight is the Sabbath when it is forbidden to carry money. Empty your pockets and put your money in the collection plates."

The Saving of Lives

Jewish law provides for emergencies. If a person is seriously ill, not only is it permissible to violate the Sabbath for his sake but it is a duty to do so. The Talmud states: "The Sabbath may be desecrated for one who is seriously ill so that he may be preserved to observe many Sabbaths" (Shabbat 151b). The problem of determining what constitutes an emergency has been the source of a number of clever stories.

THE SAVING OF A COW

One Sabbath afternoon, Hershele Ostropoler visited the rabbi. He happened to look out of the window and then turned to the rabbi and asked:

"Rabbi, is it permissible to save a cow from drowning on the Sabbath?"

"Hershele, you should know that it is forbidden."

"Are you certain, rabbi, that nothing can be done to spare the life of an animal?"

"Certainly not."

"Rabbi, I'm sure that you'll regret your decision."

"I don't understand why you question my decision. Of course, Hershele, under certain circumstances it's permissible to save an animal."

Peering through the window again, Hershele said:

"Well, rabbi, in any case, it's too late now. I just saw your cow drown."

THE LAW OF BLEEDING ON THE SABBATH

A *Yeshivah* student requested rabbinical ordination from Rabbi Solomon Kluger of Brody. He had prepared himself thoroughly for the examination and felt confident that he could answer any questions that the rabbi might ask. When the rabbi had presented some unusually difficult questions of law to the student and found that he was well qualified, he asked one more question:

"What is the law about a person who cuts his finger on the Sabbath and blood is gushing forth?"

"I'll be able to answer this question," the cautious student replied, "if you'll allow me an opportunity to refer to the Code of Law."

"Oh, I'm sorry, my son. You cannot be ordained as a rabbi," the sage said. "While you are looking up the law, the man could bleed to death."

REWARD FOR PROFANATION OF THE DAY OF REST

Elijah, the Gaon of Wilna, the outstanding rabbi of his time, once urged a leading and pious Jew of the community to travel to a distant city to intercede for a group of Jews who were facing a disastrous governmental decree. His mission proved successful, but in the course of his urgent efforts the Jewish leader was forced to desecrate the holy Sabbath. Sorely distressed, he experienced pangs of guilt for his unwilling violation.

Returning to Wilna, he reported to the Gaon and asked him how he should repent for the sin of desecrating the day of rest.

Elijah said to him:

"I'll make an exchange with you. I'll give you the merit of a Sabbath that I observed most scrupulously if you'll transfer to me the reward of that Sabbath that you profaned."

A Fireman to the Rescue!

One Sabbath a Jew came to Hayyim Joseph Sonnenfeld, a distinguished rabbi of Jerusalem, and informed the sage that his neighbor had just lit a fire and was cooking. Immediately, the rabbi donned his Sabbath coat and *Streimel* and hastened to the home of the Jew who dared to violate the sacred day of rest in the Holy City. The transgressor saw the rabbi approaching his home and quickly extinguished the fire. The rabbi rushed into the house without knocking and looked about but naturally didn't see any fire burning. The Sabbath violator, who also had no respect for the learned and pious patriarch, said indignantly:

"It's certainly impolite to enter a person's home without knocking on the door!"

"I thought that there was no need to stand on ceremony," the rabbi said. "I was told that there was a fire in your house and I rushed in to save you."

For the Sake of the Critically Ill

One day Sholom Aleichem and a few of his writer friends decided to pay a visit to Rabbi Samuel Mohilever, an early Zionist of the nineteenth century. As they approached his home in a horse driven carriage, they saw the rabbi seated on his porch, studying the Talmud. To their surprise, he was attired in his Sabbath clothes. It suddenly dawned upon them that it was indeed the Sabbath. Sholom Aleichem and the other authors felt embarrassed and ashamed that they had publicly violated the Sabbath in the presence of this saint whom they truly respected.

Seeing them and sensing their embarrassment, Rabbi Mohilever said:

"Friends, I understand the shame that you are experiencing and which is causing you to become quite ill. As you know, those who are critically ill are permitted to violate the Sabbath. Come in and refresh yourselves."

THE GIFTS OF THE SABBATH

A scoffer used the following logic to justify his violation of the Sabbath on the grounds that he desired to live long:

"The Talmud says, 'God said to the Jews: I have a precious gift in my treasury and Sabbath is its name.' As I refuse to accept this gift I am assured of long life, as it is written in the Bible: 'And he who hates gifts will live.' "

The Observance of the Sabbath

Ahad Ha-am said: "More than Israel has kept the Sabbath, the Sabbath has kept Israel."
The Sabbath laws of the Bible and the fences

*built around them by the rabbis are intended
to reflect the Jew's concern for perpetuating
the Sabbath so that he, in turn, may live on.
Tradition tells us that included in the rewards
for Sabbath observance is the redemption of
Israel. In accordance with Jewish thought,
the rabbis have interpreted the laws of the
Sabbath to make them practicable. Thus,
despite economic and social handicaps, Jews
in all generations have found it possible to
joyously observe the day of rest.*

COMBING ONE'S HAIR

One Sabbath a rabbi met Baron Wilhelm Rothschild of Frankfort, who was a God-fearing Jew. Observing that the hair on the baron was unkempt because of
the prohibition of combing one's hair on the Sabbath,
the rabbi remarked:

"You should know that it's permissible for you to
comb your hair on the Sabbath. After all, you need to
deal constantly with the government."

The baron said:

"Rabbi, this dispensation doesn't apply to me. I
don't need to deal with the government. The government needs to deal with me."

A PRECIOUS CIGARETTE

Rabbi Simon Schreiber, a member of the Austrian
parliament, was invited to a reception at the palace of
Emperor Francis Joseph. The reception was held on a
Saturday. When the emperor honored his guests by

offering them his monogrammed cigarettes, everyone naturally accepted. Noticing that Rabbi Simon was not smoking, the emperor asked him:

"Perhaps the brand of cigarette that I smoke is not to your liking?"

Unwilling to embarrass the emperor by telling him that a Jew should not smoke on the Sabbath, the rabbi—diplomat that he was—promptly responded:

"On the contrary, Your Excellency. The gift of the emperor is so precious to me that I will not dissipate it in smoke."

CHILDREN'S RESPONSIBILITY

"Why are you so concerned that your children should scrupulously observe the Sabbath while you yourself are so lax?" a woman asked her neighbor.

"Because," her neighbor replied, "it is written in the Torah: 'And the children of Israel shall keep the Sabbath.' "

THE SUPERSTITION OF THE SABBATH

A Jew had just become a proud grandfather. He immediately went to purchase an amulet for the newborn. To his chagrin, he found a small sign on the door: "Closed for the Sabbath."

With grim determination, the new grandfather hastened to the shopkeeper's home and told the merchant that he wanted to purchase an amulet for the infant. He would even pay the merchant something extra for the trouble of opening his store.

"I'm sorry," the shopkeeper said. "I don't engage in business on the Sabbath."

The disappointed grandfather fumed:

"Do you mean to tell me that you won't sell me an amulet for my grandchild because of your superstition about observing the Sabbath?"

Hot Tea for the Day of Delight

One cold, wintry Sabbath afternoon, Reb Avraham was seated in his living room studying the weekly portion of the Pentateuch and yearning for a glass of hot tea. His physical need overcame his spiritual preoccupation and he arose and entered the kitchen. Disappointed in finding the samovar empty, he said to his Polish maid:

"If today were not the Sabbath when I'm forbidden to ask you to perform any labor, I would ask you to make me a glass of hot tea."

So saying, he returned to his studies.

The maid took the hint and shortly brought him a glass of steaming, hot tea.

Lights Out

A *Masmid,* who slept very little so that he would have as much time as possible to devote to his studies, arose in the middle of a Friday night during the winter to pore over his books. Disappointed at finding that the Sabbath candles were no longer burning, he went outside to seek a *Shabbos Goy,* a Gentile, to rekindle the lights.

Pleasantly surprised to find a homeless beggar trying

to warm himself by standing close to the house, the *Masmid* invited him to come in for a drink of whiskey. Of course, he would not violate the Sabbath by directly requesting a Gentile to do something for him. The beggar eagerly accepted the unexpected invitation.

As the *Masmid* and the beggar entered the house, the learned one hinted that it would be difficult for him to find the bottle in the darkness. The anxious beggar kindled the lights without further ado. The host then poured a good, stiff drink for the beggar who imbibed it in measured sips. The *Masmid* waited impatiently for his guest to finish and leave so that he could study by the light of the candles. Warmed by the drink, the beggar thanked his host and, as he turned to leave, blew out the candles, throwing the room back into pitch darkness.

STEALING ON THE SABBATH

A Jewish wine dealer came to the city to purchase a supply of wine for Passover from a kosher wine wholesaler. Arriving shortly before the Sabbath, he decided that the best way to safeguard his money over the Sabbath was to hide it among the wine barrels in the merchant's cellar. He was certain that no one would go near the barrels on the holy day.

After *Havdalah* the following night, the visiting dealer went down into the cellar for his money. To his horror, he found that it was missing. He sought out the wholesaler and accused him of stealing the money. The merchant heatedly denied the charge. Words nearly led to blows. Finally, they agreed to go to the rabbi and present their case.

The rabbi listened carefully to both sides and then issued his decree:

"According to the testimony we know that the money was left in the wine cellar. It's also evident that the money couldn't have been taken by a Jew because it was the Sabbath. Therefore, the money must have been stolen by a non-Jew who, in the process of searching for it, would have been compelled to touch the wine barrels. The law is clear: any wine that's touched by a non-Jew is unsuitable for use. I, therefore, order that an announcement be made in all the synagogues that the wine of the wholesaler is not *Kosher* and may not be used."

When the merchant heard the decree of the rabbi and realized the loss that he would be compelled to sustain, he immediatcly confessed that he stole the money.

Desecration of the Sabbath

The modern laxity of traditional observances resulting from the industrial revolution and the pervasive ignorance of laws and customs have caused a breach in the "cornerstone of Judaism," the designation given to the Sabbath by Hayyim Nahman Bialik. Many Jews have failed to comprehend that the prohibitions relating to work on the Sabbath are not restrictions, in the ordinary sense, but rather safeguards for a relaxing, peaceful and enjoyable day. The lack of any appreciation of the values of the Sabbath is revealed in many stories. The abundance of tales in this area may also reflect the need to remonstrate with violators because of the severity of Sabbath desecration.

EXTINGUISHING THE SABBATH CANDLES

Passing the home of his grandparents late one Friday night, Ephraim Greidiger, a nineteenth century legendary character of Galicia, was surprised to see lights burning inside. He entered the house and asked the old folks why they were still awake. They explained that for some unknown reason the Sabbath candles were still burning and they were afraid to go to bed lest a fire break out. As observant Jews, they could not blow out the candles.

Ephraim immediately thought of an easy solution.

"I think you'll be able to go to sleep now without desecrating the holy Sabbath," he said, placing himself opposite the candles. Taking a deep breath, he emitted a puff as he pronounced the first syllable of the following sentence:

"*Pu*-rim will soon be here!"

He continued:

"I hope you'll have *Hamantashen* for me on *Pu*-rim."

Each puff that accompanied the *Pu* extinguished a candle, plunging the house into darkness.

STEALING FOR THE SABBATH ESCORTS

When Rabbi Akiva Eger accepted the rabbinical post in Posen, he was greatly disturbed to learn that many Jews in the community attended the theater on Friday nights. During a sermon on this subject, he remarked:

"I was never able to understand the talmudical state-ment that there may be cities wherein 'the majority of thieves are Jews.' Now I know that this applies to Posen. In this city many Jews attend the theater on Friday night. We know that on the Sabbath eve every Jew is escorted by two angels and for them he doesn't buy any tickets for the theater."

No Need for a Shabbos Goy

A pious bride was observing the first Sabbath with her groom who happened to be lax in his adherence to Jewish tradition.

After the Sabbath meal, the groom extinguished the lights in the dining room. Shocked at this flagrant violation of the Sabbath, the bride berated him. The groom attempted to pacify her:

"My beloved, we're truly meant for each other. Don't you see? Since you married me you'll never need a *Shabbos Goy*."

The Mitzvah of Soccer Playing

A group of Tel Avivians were seated in a café on Allenby Street discussing sports. The main topic was soccer.

Jonathan raised the question:

"Is it a *Mitzvah*, a good deed, or a sin to play soccer on the Sabbath?"

"Our ancestors never played football even on week-days . . ." David began to explain.

Jonathan interrupted:

"What you say proves that it's a *Mitzvah* to play football on the Sabbath. Our ancestors were punished and they all died."

A Sin in Tel Aviv

An American tourist in Israel was spending his first Sabbath at a hotel in Tel Aviv. Saturday morning, as he was on his way to the synagogue, he noticed a Jew smoking a cigarette. Amazed to witness this public desecration of the Sabbath in the all-Jewish city, the new arrival approached the smoker and rebuked him:

"It's a sin to smoke on the Sabbath!"

The other sharply retorted:

"You're mistaken. It's a *Mitzvah* and not a sin. Didn't the prophet Isaiah say: 'And you shall call the Sabbath a delight'? Let me tell you that there's no greater delight than smoking after a heavy Sabbath meal."

Returning from the synagogue to the hotel, the tourist saw many Jews riding in automobiles. He approached a passer-by and asked:

"Don't the Jews of Tel Aviv rest on the Sabbath? If so, how can they ride today?"

The passer-by replied nonchalantly:

"You misunderstand the intentions of our local Jews. All week they walk and rush about until they're completely exhausted. By riding today they truly enjoy Sabbath rest."

When the American returned to his hotel, he chanted the *Kiddush* and began to partake of the Sabbath meal that was set before him. Finding the soup too sharp for his taste, he called the waitress and requested her to bring a little water so that he might dilute the soup.

The waitress indignantly refused and scolded the guest:

"It's a sin to spoil this delicious soup by putting water in it!"

The tourist sighed and mused to himself:

"Now, I know what's a sin in Tel Aviv."

When Is the Sabbath?

A father called for his son at the children's house of a *Kibbutz* in the Emek.

Father: Come, my son, let's go for a walk.

Son: Do you have Sabbath today?"

Father: No, son. I have just finished my day's work. I had my Sabbath yesterday.

Son: When will mother have her Sabbath?

Father: Tomorrow.

Son: What day is today?

Father: Today is Sabbath.

Son: Tell me the truth, father. What's today?

Father: I am telling you the truth. Today's the Sabbath.

Son: Before you said that yesterday was your Sabbath and tomorrow will be mother's Sabbath. Whose Sabbath is today?

Father: Why don't you understand? Today is the Sabbath of all Jewish people.

Son: Are you and mother Jewish?

Father: Of course!

Son: Father, do the Jewish people always observe the Sabbath on the Sabbath?

Father: Yes . . . No . . . Son, let's go for a walk.

THE FEAR OF GOD

A *Hasid* intercepted a Jew carrying a walking stick on the Sabbath. In a harsh, scolding tone, he rebuked the desecrator of the holy day, saying:

"Don't you have any fear of God that you dare to carry a cane in a public place on the Sabbath?"

The Jew rejoined:

"It's precisely because I fear God that I carry a stick."

THE PRICE OF SABBATH TRANSGRESSION

The rabbi heard that one of his congregants, whom he had known to be an observant Jew, had taken to gambling and even played cards on the Sabbath.

The next time that the rabbi encountered this particular congregant, he asked him if the rumor he had heard were true. The shamefaced man readily confessed. He asked the rabbi how he might atone for his transgression.

The rabbi said:

"To make true repentance for your violation of the Sabbath you must make a substantial contribution to the synagogue."

"Rabbi, if you only knew," the gambler hesitatingly pleaded, "how much this transgression has already cost me!"

WHAT NO JEW OR NON-JEW HAS DONE

A youth who had strayed from the path of Judaism was being taken to task by his devout father. The latter threatened to discontinue his son's allowance if he continued in his God-forsaken ways.

"If you do that, father, I'll do something that no Jew or non-Jew has ever done," said the rebellious son.

"What . . . what'll you do?"

"I'll put on *Tephillin* on the Sabbath!"

A Devout Jew

A prosperous young man had just moved into his own home in a new suburban community. The local rabbi duly paid him a courtesy call and invited him to join the congregation. The young man not only readily agreed to become an active member; he also made every effort to impress upon the rabbi his personal interest in Judaism. Extremely pleased to have such a staunch and devout Jew in his midst as there were so few in the suburb, the rabbi urged the newcomer to attend the daily morning services as it was difficult to secure the required *Minyan*.

"I'm sorry," the newcomer apologized, "but I'm too busy during the week and I haven't any time to pray. I want you to know, however, that every Saturday I put on *Tephillin*."

Tell It to the Chaplain!

At Camp Upton a Jewish private reported late for the morning drill. When the sergeant asked him the reason for his lateness, the private explained that it was the Sabbath and he had to put on phylacteries. The Irish sergeant, who was raised in a Jewish neighborhood, knew that Jews do not use *Tephillin* on the Sabbath. He therefore ordered the private:

"Report to Chaplain Goldberg and tell him your story!"

INTER-FAITH PENITENCE

A Jewish farmer, having lost the reckoning of the days of the week, rode into a nearby city one Saturday morning in the belief that it was Friday.

A Jew, on the way to the synagogue, yelled at the farmer:

"How dare you publicly violate the Sabbath!"

Greatly distressed, the farmer said:

"If today is the Sabbath, then yesterday must've been Friday."

"Certainly," the Jew rejoined.

The farmer heaved a deep sigh and said:

"I'm responsible for the sin of my Catholic servant. Yesterday, I gave him meat to eat."

A JEW RIDES ON THE SABBATH!

Hayyim was taking his Sabbath afternoon stroll. As he passed the railroad station, a train arrived and a passenger, who was obviously a Jew, alighted.

Hayyim emitted a penetrating shriek:

"*Oi!* A plague on me! A Jew rides on the Sabbath!"

The Jewish passenger unabashedly approached Hayyim and said to him:

"Ten plagues on you! There are nine other Jews on the train."

A HOLY OCCUPATION ON THE SABBATH

An architectural firm hired a young architect who was ambitious and hard-working. One Monday morning the new member of the firm reported to the Jewish owner that during the weekend he was able to complete the plans for an apartment house as he worked in the office on Saturday.

Instead of appreciating the industriousness and loyalty of his employee, the owner waxed angry. He advised the young man that henceforth he should never come into the office on Saturday as the firm was Sabbath-observing.

Some weeks later, the employee learned that his boss had been working in the office on a Saturday also. Deeply perplexed, he hesitatingly asked:

"Not that I mind but why is it proper for you to work on Saturday and not right for me to do so?"

"My work was different," the owner explained. "I was drawing plans for a new synagogue building."

THE HANDS OF ESAU

One Sabbath Jacob Levy went to pay a visit to his rabbi. Upon arriving at the rabbi's home, he used the door-knocker to announce his presence. Amazed that anyone would violate the Sabbath by using the knocker, the rabbi approached the door and inquired:

"Who's there?"

"Jacob," came the reply.

Opening the door, the rabbi quoted the patriarch Isaac:

"The voice is the voice of Jacob but the hands are the hands of Esau."

Doing Business on the Day of Rest

A stranger in town on the Sabbath was surprised to see a bearded Jew standing in front of a clothing store, obviously seeking customers. He approached the storekeeper and asked him:

"How can a Jew with a beard do business on the Sabbath?"

"If I sell a forty dollar suit for twenty dollars, do you call that doing business?" the storekeeper wanted to know.

Stores Open on Saturday

A Jewish farmer once visited a big city. Upon his return home, his neighbors gathered to hear an eyewitness report on the wonders of the large metropolis. He told them of the strange and marvellous sights he had seen. He also felt compelled, however, to render a distressing report on the Jews he had met in the city:

"The Jews there aren't Jews at all! On the Sabbath their stores are open."

One of the neighbors naïvely asked:

"Are they crazy? What good is it to have their stores open on Saturday when it's forbidden to do business?"

Smoking on the Sabbath

A Jew, seen smoking on the Sabbath, was taken to task for his obvious violation of Jewish law.

"Don't criticize me," he said, haughtily. "I already asked the rabbi."

"Yes, and what did the rabbi say?"

"What should the rabbi say? The rabbi said that it's forbidden."

THE JEWS ARE A WONDERFUL PEOPLE

One Sabbath afternoon Rabbi Levi Isaac of Berditchev, the ardent defender of Israel of the eighteenth century, met a Jew puffing on a cigarette. The rabbi inquired:

"Don't you know that today is the Sabbath?"

"Yes, I know," the Jew answered truthfully.

"Don't you know that it's forbidden to smoke on the Sabbath?" Levi Isaac probed further.

"Yes, I know," the Jew replied.

"Are you ill, God forbid, that you must smoke to assuage your pain?"

"No, rabbi. I'm quite well, thank you."

Levi Isaac then raised his eyes heavenward and exclaimed:

"Master of the Universe! See what a wonderful people the Jews are. Even when a Jew commits a sin, he doesn't lie."

Continuing his Sabbath stroll, the rabbi encountered yet another Jew smoking. When he saw the rabbi approaching, he quickly hid his cigarette behind his back.

The charitable rabbi once again lifted his gaze on high, saying:

"Master of the Universe! See what a wonderful

people the Jews are. Even when a Jew commits a sin, he is also ashamed."

THE PLACE FOR A TRUTHFUL MAN

Leaving the synagogue after the Saturday morning services, Rabbi Akiva Eger was shocked to meet one of his congregants with a lit pipe in his mouth.

"Did you forget that today is the Sabbath?" the rabbi asked.

"I won't lie to you, rabbi. I didn't forget that today is the Sabbath. I also know that it's forbidden to smoke today."

"You're indeed a man of truth and your place is in the world of eternal truth," declared the rabbi. Then he changed his tone. "I'm really surprised that you remain in this world of falsehood and deceit."

THE CURE BEFORE THE DISEASE

Rabbi Akiva Eger expressed in no uncertain terms his disapproval of a Jew whom he saw violating the Sabbath by smoking.

In an apologetic tone, the Jew said:

"I'm smoking for a cure, rabbi."

Rabbi Akiva answered:

"The Almighty always provides a cure before the disease takes effect. Now that you already have a cure, I fear that you'll be stricken with a disease."

PERMISSIVE SMOKING ON THE SABBATH

"Rabbi," a freethinker asked Meir Leibush ben Yehiel Michel, known as the Malbim, "is it possible to have a device whereby it may be permitted to smoke a cigarette on the Sabbath?"

"Yes," responded the rabbi. "If you'll make a change so that your method of smoking on the Sabbath will be different from that of the week days."

"Well, what kind of a change would you suggest?"

"Smoke the cigarette with the burning end in your mouth!" the rabbi replied.

TOLERATING SMOKE

A leader of the Hapoel Hamizrachi was invited to address a non-religious workers' group in Tel Aviv on a Saturday afternoon. As he entered the meeting place, he found it filled with smoke. He immediately told the chairman that he would not participate in a meeting where the Sabbath was being publicly desecrated. The chairman politely but urgently requested him to remain and then addressed the audience:

"Kindly refrain from smoking as our guest speaker cannot tolerate smoke." He proceeded with a warm and lengthy introduction of the speaker.

The Hapoel Hamizrachi leader began his address with an expression of appreciation to the chairman for his flattering introduction. Then he said:

"The chairman was mistaken in one point. I can tolerate smoke but God doesn't tolerate it."

NO SUBSTITUTE POSSIBLE

Late one Friday night, Reuben Asher Braudes, the celebrated writer, was drinking beer and smoking cigarettes in a tavern. The hour for closing came and the Jewish owner of the tavern started to put out the lights. When Braudes saw him extinguish a lamp, he censured him:

"Today is the Sabbath!"

"Are you also not obligated to observe the Sabbath?" the perplexed man asked. "Why are you smoking?"

"My situation is very different than yours," explained Braudes. "You can have a Gentile extinguish your lights on the Sabbath but I can't have anyone smoke for me."

THE RIGHT TO DIFFER

A pious Jew became mentally ill and was committed to an insane asylum. One Sabbath he absolutely refused to eat the noon meal because it was cooked that day. As a result of the strenuous objections he expressed to being forced to violate the Sabbath, the doctor gave orders to serve him uncooked food to quiet him down.

Later in the day the doctor observed the Jew smoking a pipe. The medico approached him and reprovingly said:

"You refused to eat food that was cooked on Saturday and now I see you smoking."

The Jew, with a gleam in his eye, declared:

"Doctor, you know that I'm crazy!"

EXEMPT FROM SABBATH OBSERVANCE

An elderly, bearded Jew, strolling in the park on Saturday afternoon and enjoying a cigar, saw a group of Jewish children playing ball. He called to them in a harsh tone:

"Children, stop playing ball! Today's the Sabbath!"

A passerby, who could not help hearing this sharp command, politely said to the patriarch:

"I'm amazed at you. Why are you so concerned about the questionable violation of the Sabbath by these small children while you yourself don't hesitate to desecrate the Sabbath publicly by smoking?"

"As I'm an old man, Sabbath observance doesn't apply to me," the venerable one explained. "It's written in the Torah: 'And the children of Israel shall keep the Sabbath.' As you can readily see, I'm far from being a child."

FORGETFUL STUDENTS

Four *Yeshivah* students were seen smoking together in a room on the Sabbath. Summoned by the head of the seminary to answer for their flagrant violation of Jewish law, the students attempted to find excuses for their actions. Each one gave a different excuse.

"I forgot that I'm a Jew."

"I forgot that it was the Sabbath."

"I forgot that it's forbidden to smoke on the Sabbath."

"I forgot to draw down the window shades."

SABBATH PLEASURE

A wealthy Jew, well-known for his charitable ways, was always seeking to perform good deeds. Learning that a poverty-stricken resident of the town smoked on the Sabbath, the rich man sent for the sinning pauper and made him this generous offer:

"If you'll stop smoking on the Sabbath, I'll give you a weekly allowance of one ruble."

The poor man paused for only a moment to consider the proposition and immediately said:

"Oh, no! For a ruble I'll not spoil my Sabbath pleasure."

AN INTENTIONAL MIX-UP

On the first day of Passover Rabbi Akiva Eger met a Jew who was smoking. The rabbi, who had reason to suspect that the Jew also smoked on the Sabbath, greeted him with a hearty *"Gut Shabbos!"*

"Rabbi, today is Passover. It's not the Sabbath," the Jew said, surprised.

"Is that so?" the rabbi sarcastically rejoined. "Well, I saw you smoking so I assumed that today is the Sabbath."

SABBATH TRANSPORTATION

A newly-arrived immigrant in New York was taking a Sabbath stroll when, to his amazement, he saw his cousin alight from a bus. Dashing over to his cousin, he heatedly berated him:

"Shame on you! How dare you take a bus ride on the Sabbath?"

The cousin answered impatiently:

"You're really a greenhorn. That was a Sabbath bus. If you'll look inside the vehicle, you'll see a sign reading 'No Smoking.' This notice is a reminder to the passengers that today is the Sabbath when smoking is forbidden."

AN ATHEIST IGNORES THE LAW

A young Jew, anxious to take a smoke on the Sabbath but ashamed to do so either at home or in the street, walked to the outskirts of the town. Indulging himself to his heart's content, he passed by an army ammunition dump.

The soldier on guard duty called to him:

"Hey, there! Don't you know it's forbidden to smoke!"

The young man haughtily asserted:

"I'm an atheist. I don't believe in such nonsense."

AN IMPOSSIBLE SITUATION

The elders of the community, making an unannounced Sabbath visit to Abraham Isaac Landau, a leading *Maskil*, were dumbfounded to find him smoking a pipe. Before they could recover from the shock, Landau unabashedly said:

"Please come back in an hour."

Still at a loss for words, the elders hastily departed. They returned an hour later and were even more stunned this time. Landau was wrapped up in his *Talis* and *Tephillin*.

One of the elders perplexedly asked:

"Why have you donned *Tephillin* on the Sabbath?"

Landau replied with an innocent air:

"How can today be the Sabbath? You yourselves saw me smoking!"

YIDDISH-READING NON-JEWS

On his first Sabbath in New York, a Polish Jewish immigrant went for a stroll through a neighborhood park. Observing many men relaxing on benches, smoking cigarettes or cigars and reading Yiddish newspapers, the immigrant said to himself:

"America is really a Jewish country. Even non-Jews here read Yiddish!"

OBSERVANT IN HIS OWN WAY

Late Saturday afternoon, a pious Jew met his new neighbor, who was smoking a cigar, and said to him:

"I thought you're an observant Jew. I'm amazed that you're already smoking so early. There are no stars in the heavens at this hour."

"Don't wonder," the neighbor responded. "You forget that I'm an astronomer. I can see stars even in the daytime."

Havdalah

On Saturday evening a separation is made between the Sabbath and the weekday by a special ceremony—Havdalah—in which blessings are recited over a cup of wine, a braided candle and a spice box. This beautiful ritual symbolizes the five senses for which joyful gratitude is offered at the beginning of the new week. With the departure of Queen Sabbath, the Jew immediately begins to look forward to greeting her again.

An Early Departure

On the way to the Sabbath afternoon services, a rabbi passed a group of young Jewish men smoking cigarettes and spoke to them with a sarcastic smile on his lips:

"Apparently, you men made *Havdalah* too early, didn't you?"

Separating the Sacred from the Secular

From sheer necessity, a Jew was forced to accept a position which compelled him to work on Saturday. Never before having violated the Sabbath, he was sorely distressed. After many sleepless nights, he hit upon a plan that would enable him to fulfill his religious obligations and maintain his position at the same time.

The following Saturday the Jew arose early, recited the Sabbath prayers and *Kiddush*, ate a meal and then chanted the *Havdalah* service, thereby bringing the Sabbath to a close. He then left the house and went to work.

Wine for Havdalah

Every Friday Hayyim bought a bottle of wine for the Sabbath. After using the wine for *Kiddush*, he never had enough for *Havdalah*. When he explained his problem to his friend Mordecai, the latter advised:

"Buy two bottles of wine—one for *Kiddush* and the other for *Havdalah*."

The next Friday Hayyim followed Mordecai's advice.

He now found, however, that he still had only enough wine for *Kiddush*.

The following week Hayyim again met Mordecai and told him his problem.

Mordecai offered another suggestion:

"Buy three bottles of wine—two for *Kiddush* and one for *Havdalah*."

Hayyim willingly accepted this second suggestion. After the Sabbath, the two friends met.

"*Nu*, Hayyim, do you now have enough wine for *Havdalah*?" Mordecai inquired.

Hayyim gleefully answered:

"Thank God. Now, I have enough. You see, I make *Havdalah* immediately after *Kiddush*."

THE CONCLUSION OF A FESTIVAL

When Shmuel's wife returned home after spending two weeks with her parents, he began to recite *Havdalah*.

His wife could not understand why he was saying this service on an ordinary weekday.

Terribly upset, she imagined that Shmuel had become mentally unbalanced during her absence. Not wishing to interrupt until he had concluded the service, she waited for the end and then nervously asked:

"Since when does one recite *Havdalah* on a weekday?"

Shmuel quietly replied:

"My dear, you know that *Havdalah* is said at the conclusion of the Sabbath and the holidays. While you were away I enjoyed a true holiday which is now concluded."

A RIDDLE

Why is the Sabbath the strongest day in the week?
Because it is the only day which is not a week (weak)
day.

FOLK PROVERBS

On Sabbath even the Sambatyon rests. (According to
a legend the Sambatyon River is turbulent during the
week but calm on the Sabbath.)

Sabbath throughout the entire world! (This happens
when peace reigns.)

Sabbath has the appearance of the next world.

On the Sabbath even the wicked in Hell have rest.

Without counting the Sabbaths and festivals. (When
one denies his age, he is told that he counts his years
"without the Sabbaths and festivals.")

Every Sabbath has its luck. (So says the poor man
who receives his Sabbath needs from the Almighty.)

A drunkard drinks wine on Friday and recites the
Kiddush over *Hallah* on Saturday.

If for the Sabbath there is no food,
On weekdays there will be nothing good.

Well-known is the Sabbath pleasure of stuffed fish
And even during the week it's no mean dish.

A Jew who is poor and meek
Dons Sabbath clothes throughout the week.
(Because he has no other clothes.)

THE DAYS OF AWE

Sounding the Shofar

CHAPTER THREE

THE DAYS OF AWE

" *THE Days of Awe"—the New Year, the Day of Atonement and the days between, when the fate of man hangs in the balance—are significantly not days of sorrow. The Jerusalem Talmud states: "A person on trial is usually dejected and has a mournful appearance but the people of Israel do otherwise. On Rosh Hashanah they wear holiday garments and enjoy festive meals. Thus they express their confidence in the mercy of God" (Rosh Hashanah 1.3). Even the most sacred day of the year—Yom Kippur—has been correctly termed by the historian Josephus as "the feast fast day."*

Tradition relates that Rabbi Abraham Joshua Heshel of Apta once said: "The Holy One, Blessed be He, wanted to provide both for the soul and the body of Israel. Therefore He gave them different festivals to meet their spiritual and bodily needs. Even the most sacred and awe-inspiring day of the year, Yom Kippur, about which the Torah states: 'And ye shall afflict your souls' (Leviticus 23.27), is preceded by the two days of Rosh Hashanah, concerning which it is written: 'Eat the fat and drink sweets, for the joy of the Lord is your strength' (Nehemiah 8.10). Moreover, on the eve of Yom

Kippur it is a duty to eat and drink, as it is written: 'Whosoever eats and drinks on the ninth (of Tishri), the Torah considers it as if he had fasted both on the ninth and tenth' (Berachot 8b)."

The Month of Elul

Preceding the High Holy Days is Elul— month of spiritual preparation. This is the time when the soul is attuned to receive the message and meaning of the great days that lie ahead. Selihos, penitential prayers, are recited daily, sometimes between midnight and dawn. Synagogue functionaries—Cantor and Ba'al Tekiah (Shofar blower)—prime themselves for the awe-inspiring services; their practice and deeds are carefully scrutinized. Innate feelings are awakened in even indifferent Jews. These stirrings, a mixture of memories, longings and yearnings for things of the spirit, move towards their culmination in attendance at synagogue. Because of their very seriousness and by reason of their fateful importance in the life of the Jew, these days become the seed-bed for quip and wit when something goes awry.

SELIHOS IN HELM

The elderly sexton of Helm complained that he was too old and weak to arise before dawn every day during the month of *Elul* to wake up the Jews for *Selihos*. It was too much of an effort for him to go from house to house and knock on all the doors of the townspeople

to summon them to the synagogue to recite the penitential prayers.

The Helmites called an emergency meeting to consider this grave situation. They examined thoroughly
all sides of the problem. After learning all the facts,
the "wise men" of Helm reached the following solution:

To spare the aging sexton from walking through the
town, the doors of all the houses would be assembled in
the synagogue. When the sexton came to the synagogue,
he would then knock on all the doors.

TYPES OF SELIHOS JEWS

Abraham Ber, the renowned free-thinker, was asked
why he did not attend the early morning *Selihos* services during the month of *Elul,* even though the sexton
walked near his house, calling "Arise for *Selihos*," and,
receiving no response, loudly beat with his fists on the
door.

The unbeliever explained:

"There are three types of *Selihos* Jews just as there
are three types of horses. A good horse goes when he is
called. Another type of horse is the one who goes when
he is beaten with a whip. There is another kind of horse
who is called and even beaten and still does not go. The
third is really not a horse at all."

REPENTANT JEWS

As Rabbi Levi Isaac of Berditchev and his sexton
were going to synagogue for the *Selihos* services, a sudden downpour of rain made them seek shelter under the
awning of a tavern. The sexton peered through one of

the windows and saw a group of Jews feasting, drinking and revelling. He impatiently urged Levi Isaac to see for himself how these Jews were behaving when they should be in the synagogue praying to God for forgiveness for their sins.

Paying no heed to the urging of the sexton, the rabbi said:

"May God bless these loyal Jews. They are surely reciting the benedictions for food and drink."

The disillusioned sexton continued to peek into the tavern and to eavesdrop.

"Woe to us, rabbi!" the sexton exclaimed. "I just heard two of the Jews boasting to each other of thefts they committed."

"See, I told you that they are observant Jews," Levi Isaac rejoicingly admonished his sexton. "They are confessing their sins before Rosh Hashanah. As you know, there are none more righteous than those who repent."

PENITENTIAL PRAYERS

Once during the penitential season, Rabbi Levi Isaac was ill. As he lay in bed, he prayed:

"Merciful Lord! I am weak and unable to arise to recite the lengthy *Selihos* prayers of forgiveness. You are strong and Your penitential prayers are brief; therefore, say: 'I have forgiven'."

REASON FOR ENVY

"I envy you," the Berditchever rabbi, hoping to lead him to repentance, told an unbeliever. "The solemn days of prayer and repentance are approaching and you will pray and repent; thus, all your sins will be considered as good deeds. You will then surely have more good deeds to your credit than I can expect."

The freethinker paused for a moment and said:

"Rabbi, if you'll wait yet another year, you'll have more reason to be envious of me."

WHY THE FISH TREMBLE

During the month of Elul, a father awoke his son early in the morning to take him to the *Selihos* services. Quite comfortable and still sleepy, the boy was reluctant to arise.

The father chided his son, saying:

"The High Holy Days are approaching and even the fish in the sea tremble with the advent of this awe-inspiring season."

The boy yawned, rolled over on his side, and, adjusting the blankets, coyly said:

"If the fish had such a luxurious bed and such warm blankets as I have, they too wouldn't tremble."

DISTURBANCE BY A SHOFAR

Abraham Isaac Kook, the late chief rabbi of Israel, was critically ill in the hospital. When the month of Elul began, he asked that the *Shofar* be blown so that he might fulfill the custom of listening to the trumpet sounds. The doctor, reluctant to comply with this request lest the noise have an adverse effect on the rabbi, tried to dissuade his patient, but in vain. The rabbi insisted that the *Shofar* be blown.

One of Rabbi Kook's pupils who was present discreetly suggested:

"If the *Shofar* is sounded in the hospital, wouldn't the other patients be disturbed?"

The pious sage immediately said:

"Maybe you're right. If that is so, do not blow the *Shofar*."

VIRTUES OF A CANTOR

A wealthy Jew came to the rabbi of his congregation with the magnanimous offer of his services as cantor for the High Holy Days. Aware of the questionable merits of the man, the rabbi frankly said to him:

"In the *Book of Psalms* there are three prayers: the Prayer of Moses (*Psalm* 90), the Prayer of David (*Psalm* 17) and the Prayer of a Poor Man (*Psalm* 2). If one is as righteous as Moses, even though he have difficulty in speech and is unable to sing, his prayer is acceptable to God. If one has a voice as sweet as David, even though he may not be as righteous, his prayer too is acceptable. If one is poor and prays with a chastened and broken heart, even though he may not be as righteous as Moses nor possess a voice as sweet as David's, his prayer is also acceptable."

The rabbi paused and then continued:

"But you unfortunately do not possess any of these virtues. You do not perform righteous deeds, your voice is not sweet and you do not even have the merit of being poor."

A Required Examination

On the eve of Rosh Hashanah, Mordecai of Nad-
vorna, a sage of the nineteenth century, stopped a cantor
who was obviously in a great hurry.

"Why are you rushing so?" the rabbi asked.

The cantor politely replied:

"I must examine the *Mahzor* and put the Rosh Hashanah prayers in the proper order."

Mordecai paused momentarily and then said, with a
smile:

"You know well that the *Mahzor* is the same that you
used last year. You had instead better examine your
deeds of the past year and try to put yourself in proper
order."

"Behold, I am Poor"

A prosperous business man who had important financial connections in many large cities settled in a suburban community. Hoping to enlist his support for the
new, struggling congregation, the local rabbi paid him
a visit and urged him to attend the services on the New
Year and Day of Atonement. He spoke eloquently of
the inspiring services and of the wonderful qualities of
the congregation's cantor.

"When our cantor chants 'Behold, I am poor,' the
entire congregation trembles with awe," the rabbi declared.

The wealthy man was not impressed with this particular virtue of the cantor and remarked:

"I'm not a cantor. My voice is indeed very weak. Yet

if I should merely whisper 'Behold, I am poor,' people in distant cities will tremble with fear."

Choosing a Shofar Blower

Rabbi Levi Isaac was examining a number of candidates for the blowing of the *Shofar* on Rosh Hashanah. He asked each one:

"What will be your thoughts while you blow the *Shofar?*"

The Berditchever rabbi was dissatisfied with the variety of pious thoughts expressed by the candidates until one of them said:

"Rabbi, I'm a simple and poor Jew. I've a daughter who has long ago reached the age for marriage but I am unable to provide a dowry for her. When I will blow the *Shofar*, I will bear my daughter in mind. I will think: 'Merciful One! I am fulfilling the commandments that you have ordained. Hearken to the sound of the *Shofar* requesting you to fulfill your obligation of providing a dowry for my daughter.' "

The pure and sincere honesty of this Jew appealed to Levi Isaac and he engaged him to sound the *Shofar*.

A Commandant Appoints a Shofar Blower

It occurred to an ignorant but affluent Jew who was not particularly regarded for his piety that he would very much like the honor of blowing the *Shofar* on the approaching New Year in the town's principal synagogue. Realizing full well that the leaders of the Jewish community would be unwilling to permit him to perform a function reserved only for the most learned and most pious, the rich Jew appealed to the District Commandant, with whom he was on intimate terms, for his intervention. The Jew stated his request:

"My lord, there is a tradition among the Jews that on the New Year a trumpet is sounded in the synagogue and I would be indebted to you if you will order the trustees of the congregation to invite me to perform this honor."

The commandant assured him that his will would be done. Thereupon he summoned the trustees and ordered them to have his wealthy friend serve as the trumpet blower on New Year. The trustees respectfully explained that this sacred function may be performed only by one whose reputation for scholarship and God-fearing qualities is well established. The official was loath to listen to their explanations. The trustees pleaded in vain as he remained obdurate. Finally, one trustee suggested:

"Perhaps, you'll be kind enough to permit us to have our regular *Shofar* blower on the New Year and your friend can sound the trumpet on the Day of Atonement?"

Not anxious to incite the Jewish community unnecessarily, yet perceiving a way of asserting his authority and simultaneously satisfying his friend, the commandant readily agreed to the new proposal. With expressions of profuse gratitude, the delegation departed in high spirit.

The rich Jew learned of the agreement reached between the leaders of the congregation and the commandant. Sorely agitated, he hurried to the official and asked why he had allowed himself to be dissuaded from his original decision.

"I've kept my promise to you," the official responded. "You'll blow the trumpet in the synagogue. It will not be on your New Year but on the Day of Atonement. I felt certain that it would make no difference to you."

"Unfortunately, that isn't so," the frustrated Jew whined. "The *Shofar* is sounded one hundred times on each of the two days of the New Year but on the Day of Atonement it is blown only once."

"You're a fool," the commandant laughed. "When the *Shofar* is in your hands, who will stop you from blowing it as much as you like!"

No NEED FOR A SHOFAR

The newly-elected president of the synagogue had completed arrangements for the employment for the High Holy Days of a cantor who was also to be responsible for the entire service. On the eve of Rosh Hashanah the cantor telephoned to the president and asked him:

"Do you have a *Shofar*?"

The president replied:

"I don't need a chauffeur. I drive my own car."

IS A SHOFAR A TRUMPET?

A poor Jew, charged with stealing a *Shofar* from a synagogue, was brought into magistrate's court.

"What are you charged with stealing?" the magistrate inquired.

"A *Shofar*," the suspect replied.

"A *Shofar*! What's that?" the jurist asked.

The poor man, perplexed and unable to explain what a *Shofar* was, couldn't answer.

Angered by this silent defiance, the magistrate threatened to hold the frightened Jew in contempt of court if he continued in his refusal to give a proper explanation of a *Shofar*.

The defendant finally attempted to pacify the jurist and said:

"A *Shofar* is a trumpet."

"Why didn't you explain it immediately?" the magistrate demanded.

"How could I say such a thing? Do you believe, Your Honor, that a *Shofar* is really a trumpet?"

SEPARATE PEWS FOR MAN AND WIFE

During the week prior to the High Holy Days, a meek-looking man called at a Temple to reserve seats.

"Please give me two seats for my wife and myself but not near each other," he told the chairman of the Temple's seating committee.

Astonished at this unusual request, the chairman took the liberty of inquiring:

"Don't you want to sit next to your wife?"

"No," the man frankly admitted. "I'm afraid that my wife may hear me recite the confession of my sins."

ROOM FOR ONE MORE

Rabbi: I can understand that there may be sound reasons why you absent yourself from the synagogue throughout the entire year, but you certainly can find time to attend on the High Holy Days.

Absentee congregant: I might be able to find the time but I still won't attend the synagogue on those days as there are so many hypocrites who come on Rosh Hashanah and Yom Kippur.

Rabbi: Don't let that deter you. There is always room for one more.

CALENDAR REFORM

At the height of the severest austerity in Israel it was rumored in Tel Aviv that the Minister of Supply and Rationing had prepared an order proclaiming that the Jews must observe only one day of Rosh Hashanah and two days of Yom Kippur.

Prayer on Rosh Hashanah

Prayer rightfully assumes a central place in the scheme of Rosh Hashanah and the liturgy for these days is embodied in the Mahzor. However, ample room is always allowed for the addition of original prayers emanating from the heart of man. One who believed intensely in original invocations and intercessions was the Hasidic rabbi, Levi Isaac of Berditchev (1740–1809). His emphasis was on "the higher fear," leading to the higher enjoyment and the higher love. His life was devoted to warm-hearted and ecstatic love of God and Israel. The tales told about him reveal his saintly character.

UNDERSTANDING PRAYER

Rabbi Levi Isaac of Berditchev was accustomed to preach to his congregation before the blowing of the

Shofar on Rosh Hashanah. One year he told the following incident to strengthen the faith of his congregants in the efficacy of their prayers:

"Once I was lodging in an inn where many Jews had come for the market day. I arose early to join in the morning services with my fellow-Jews who were there for business. I was shocked to observe how they rushed through the prayers, mispronouncing half of the words and swallowing the other half. With the conclusion of the service, I began to speak to these merchants thus: 'Ba . . me . . ba . . ta . . .' They naturally stared at me in astonishment and undoubtedly wondered if I had become insane. I explained to them:

" 'The manner in which I have just spoken to you was very similar to the way that you spoke to God.'

"One of the business men replied to me:

" 'A baby in his cradle utters syllables that are completely meaningless even to sages, but the mother and father know the spirit of their infant and understand every utterance of his mouth. Even if you, rabbi, didn't comprehend our prayers, I have every confidence in the Almighty that he knows our thoughts and intentions.'

"This merchant was right," concluded the rabbi. "He evinced more faith in God than I did. Therefore, my friends, know that on this sacred day even the prayers of those who are unable to worship properly will be answered."

COMPOSING PRAYERS

Levi Isaac stood by the reader's table prepared to sound the *Shofar*. The congregation waited patiently for him to commence blowing. After a long while, the sexton hesitatingly approached Levi Isaac and asked the cause for the unanticipated delay.

The rabbi whispered to the sexton:

"A stranger is seated near the door of the synagogue. Raised among non-Jews, he never learned to pray. However, he has just told God:

" 'Lord of the Universe, You understand the true meaning of prayers and you know those that are most acceptable to you. As I know only the letters of the alphabet, I will recite them and from the letters You can compose the prayers that I should recite on this sacred day.'

"The Almighty is now preoccupied with the composition of prayers from the letters. Therefore, we must wait."

THE REASON A JEW PRAYS FOR PROSPERITY

During the Rosh Hashanah services, Levi Isaac, in his own inimitable manner, addressed the King of Kings thus:

"Almighty One, Blessed be Thy Name! Why does a Jew pray for a year of sustenance and plenty? Why does a Jew need money? When a Jew has the means he gives charity to the poor, provides for the education of his children, purchases a choice *Esrog* for Sukkos, buys beautiful clothing and tasty food to honor Your Sabbath; he also uses money to fulfill the other laws that You have commanded him. If You want the children of Israel to continue to obey Your commandments during the coming year, then You must grant them an abundance of wealth."

Rosh Hashanah on the Sabbath

On a Rosh Hashanah that coincided with the Sabbath, Rabbi Levi Isaac made this appeal to God:

"Master of the Universe! Today is the New Year when You usually inscribe the Jews either in the Book of Life or in the Book of Death. However, today is also the Sabbath. As it is forbidden to write on the Sabbath, how will it be possible for You to inscribe the Jewish people for the coming year? There is only one course open to You. If you will inscribe them for a year of life, then it will be permissible for You to write as 'the duty of saving lives supersedes the Sabbath laws.' "

No Need to Pray

A six-year-old girl accompanied her mother to the synagogue on the New Year. The mother explained to her daughter that on this holy day we pray for all the things we want during the coming year.

"Ma, can I really get everything for which I pray?" the child naïvely asked.

"Darling. You will get everything that's good for you."

"Oh, what good is that!" the girl disgustedly muttered under her breath. "I get that anyway."

A Smart Son

Hayyim's son Joey was reared according to the latest theories of child psychology. The boy was a precocious youngster without any inhibitions. He treated his father

as a pal and called him by his first name. Hayyim looked
askance at this particular habit of his son and one day
he said to his offspring:

"You know, it's disrespectful to call me Hayyim. Why
don't you change it to *Abba,* the Hebrew word for
Daddy?"

Shortly thereafter Hayyim took Joey, who was already learning to read Hebrew, to the synagogue for
the Rosh Hashanah services. When the bright son saw
in the festival prayer book *Zochrenu le-hayyim, Melech
hofetz be-hayyim* [Remember us for life, O King who
desires life], he made the necessary changes and in a
loud, clear voice intoned:

"Zochrenu le-abba, Melech hofetz be-abba . . ."

APPRECIATION OF THE CANTOR

A newly-engaged cantor used the Rosh Hashanah
service to display his vocal talents. He sang the prayers,
to his own satisfaction at least, repeating the same words
many times and prolonging the service until late in
the afternoon.

At the conclusion of the service, the cantor approached
the rabbi to wish him a happy new year and to hear
the compliments of the spiritual leader for the manner
in which he led the congregation in prayer.

The rabbi returned his greeting and added:

"It is written in the *Ethics of the Fathers:* 'The world
is based on three things—Torah, prayer and deeds of
kindness.' Blessed is our congregation which fulfills these
three requisites. I teach them the Torah; you pray for
them; and they perform deeds of kindness by listening
to both of us."

A Phenomenal Memory

Following the Rosh Hashanah morning services the cantor asked the president of the congregation if he was satisfied with the prayers. The president answered:

"Your memory is really phenomenal. You remembered all the mistakes you made last year and repeated them in exactly the same manner. That is truly a great accomplishment."

A Cantor Causes Weeping

A cantor was engaged by a congregation to officiate during the High Holy Days with the stipulation that, if his services proved satisfactory, he would be given a contract for a year. They were far from satisfactory, however. At the trustees' meeting convened to decide whether or not to continue the cantor's services, nothing but criticism was voiced. The president climaxed the series of complaints with the following observation:

"Even during the memorial services this cantor did not succeed in evoking any tears from me."

The treasurer, however, arose and admitted:

"I wept copiously . . ."

Shouts of astonishment interrupted him. When the president restored order, the treasurer continued:

"I wept copiously for the five hundred dollars we paid the cantor."

Blowing the Shofar

The blowing of the Shofar, a ram's horn, is not an easy thing. A folk proverb says: "When

the blower of the Shofar cannot perform satis-
factorily, he claims that Satan entered the
Shofar."

CONFUSING SATAN

A precocious lad's father discovered him eating before
the blowing of the *Shofar* on Rosh Hashanah. The father
rebukingly reminded his son that it was forbidden to
eat until after the *Shofar* is sounded.

The boy immediately justified his action:

"Father, I ate intentionally to confuse Satan. Satan
surely knows that it is not permissible to eat until the
Shofar sounds are heard. Now that Satan saw me eating
he will think that we have concluded the services. Thus,
he will not attempt to confound the sounding of the
Shofar and we can be assured of a good year."

Casting Sins Into the Waters

An old custom—that of symbolically casting
sins into the depth of the waters (Tashlich)—
takes place on the first afternoon of the New
Year on the banks of a body of water.

GATHERING IN SINS

Rabbi Jacob Isaac, the "Seer" of Lublin, and his
former pupil, Rabbi Naphtali Tzvi of Ropshitz, were
standing on the bank of a river reciting the *Tashlich*
service on Rosh Hashanah. When the teacher shook out
the pockets of his clothing to symbolically cast off his

sins, his modest pupil stretched forth his hands and motioned as if he was gathering in the sins.

Rabbi Jacob Isaac looked questioningly at his pupil. Naphtali explained:

"My teacher and master, I am gathering up your sins as I am certain that such sins that you have committed will be reckoned as good deeds for me."

Costly Sins

A prosperous Jew was chided by his rabbi for not going to the river to perform the prescribed *Tashlich* service on Rosh Hashanah.

The Jew attempted to justify his negligence.

"My sins cost me dearly," he told the rabbi, "and it would be a greater sin to throw them into the water."

New Year Greetings

It is customary to greet one another on New Year with the wish: "May you be written and sealed (signed) for a good year."

Written and Signed for a Good Year

On New Year the wealthy Baron Ginzberg happened to meet J. L. Gordon, the noted Hebrew author, and extended the traditional greeting that he be written and signed in the book of life for a good year.

Gordon quickly responded:

"If you will furnish the signature, I will supply the writing."

The Sabbath of Repentance

*The Sabbath of Repentance, that falls be-
tween the New Year and the Day of Atonement, is marked by special, usually lengthy, dis-
courses by the rabbi or Magid in the synagogue.
The preacher exhorts the congregants to repent
and to return to God. That these sermons
served varied purposes is evident in some of
the following stories.*

A MULTITUDE OF WORDS

A learned Jew, who was not favorably inclined towards his rabbi, listened impatiently to an exceptionally
lengthy discourse by the spiritual leader on the Sabbath
of Repentance.

When the rabbi finally concluded, the erudite Jew
turned to his neighbors and said:

"I understand why it is a practice of rabbis to deliver
unduly extended sermons on the Sabbath between Rosh
Hashanah and Yom Kippur. Our pious and virtuous
rabbis have no sins for which they can request forgiveness on the Day of Atonement. So that the Yom Kippur
prayers for atonement may not be recited in vain, they
preach at length on the Sabbath of Repentance, for it
is written in the *Book of Proverbs:* 'In the multitude of
words there wanteth not transgression.' "

UNWARRANTED HUMILIATION

On the Sabbath of Repentance a visiting *Magid*
preached a sermon in the synagogue of Rabbi Meir Hur-

witz of Tiktin, renowned for his piety. The preacher
castigated the congregants for their sins and urged them
to repent. When the severe tongue-lashing was brought
to an end, Rabbi Meir, tears rolling down his cheeks,
said to the *Magid:*

"I was deeply moved by your stirring words and I
will surely repent for my transgressions. However, I am
also sorely distressed that you found it necessary to put
me to shame before my entire congregation. Do I really
merit such treatment from you?"

Abashed, the preacher said:

"I would never humiliate you in public. I wasn't referring to you at all for you are well-known for your
piety."

Unassuaged, Rabbi Meir retorted:

"My congregants are all pious and the only one who
could be guilty of sin is myself."

CONCERN FOR BODY AND SOUL

Rabbi Israel Lipkin Salanter preached a sermon on
the Sabbath of Repentance in which he expressed this
thought:

"It is usual that a man expresses concern for his own
body and for the soul of his neighbor. He usually
doesn't worry about his own soul nor about the body
of his neighbor. The reverse should be the case if man
is to repent and earn his share in the world to come. Man
should disregard his own body and pay attention to his
soul. He also need not be concerned about the soul of
his neighbor but he should make certain to provide for
his bodily needs."

The Reward of Repentance

Preaching on the Sabbath of Repentance, a *Magid* told the following story to demonstrate the significance of the day:

"An unbeliever, who had violated every commandment of the Torah, passed away. He had never repented for his sins. Do you know what happened to his corpse? They dug a grave and buried him in unsanctified soil outside of the cemetery. Do you think he remained buried? No! Even the unholy soil did not want him and the very same day he was interred the earth thrust forth this sinner.

"When the rabbi was told what had happened, he issued an order:

" 'Throw the sinner in fire!'

"So they took the corpse and threw him into a blazing fire. Do you think the fire burned him? No! The fire refused to burn him.

"When the rabbi was informed what had happened, he advised:

" 'Throw the sinner to the dogs!'

"So they took the corpse and cast him to a pack of starving hounds. Do you think the dogs devoured him? No! The dogs refused to eat the *Treifah* corpse.

"My friends, learn well the moral of this story," the Magid concluded. "I call upon you on this Sabbath of Repentance to atone for your sins. For now you know what happens to one who does not repent.

"Brethren, if you repent, then you will be amply rewarded—the earth will take you, the fire will burn you and the dogs will devour you!"

A Prerequisite for Forgiveness

A Hebrew teacher was explaining to his class the laws of repentance. After a lengthy presentation on the methods of achieving atonement for sins, he asked his pupils:

"Who knows what to do before one is forgiven for committing a sin?"

Bright little Abe raised his hand and, when the teacher called upon him, he answered:

"First one must commit a sin."

The Penitent

By Ben-Jacob

A rich, but not a holy man,
Grew old, and to repent began;
So, to perform a pious deed
That would procure him heaven's meed,
He thought, and thought, then bade at last
His *servants* one whole day to fast.*

Kol Nidrei Evening

The Kol Nidrei ("All vows") prayer, preceding the evening service of the Day of Atonement, is chanted with intense feeling of solemnity and joy. The melody, a web woven of mingled emotions, creates a unique atmosphere of nostalgia, yearning and hope that makes Kol Nidrei the year's most solemn moment. It is

* J. Chotzner, *Hebrew Humour and Other Essays* (London, 1905).

*this solemnity and significance—so fraught
with emotional tension—that have been the
source of several humane stories.*

THE MISSING RABBI

The congregation, assembled in the synagogue for the
Kol Nidrei service scheduled to begin before sunset,
waited rather impatiently for the arrival of their rabbi,
Israel Lipkin Salanter. The sun had already set over
the tree-tops. The Jews were bewildered for their saintly
rabbi always came to the synagogue very early on the
eve of the holiest night in the year.

Fearing that some tragedy might have befallen the
rabbi, the congregants left the house of worship and
sought to locate him.

Rabbi Israel was not found in his home. The streets
and alleys were searched in vain. As they were about to
give up hope of locating the rabbi, the sexton noticed
a light burning in a window of a shack and he peered
inside. To his amazement, he saw the saintly sage seated
by the side of a cradle, rocking it gently.

Dashing into the shack, the sexton angrily exclaimed:

"Rabbi, the entire congregation is looking for you.
The time for beginning the *Kol Nidrei* service is already
past. What are you doing here?"

Motioning to the sexton to be quiet, the rabbi softly
rejoined:

"On my way to the synagogue long before sunset, I
passed by this house and heard the crying of a baby.
Receiving no reply when I knocked on the door, I entered and observed that the baby was alone. It was evident that the infant's mother had gone to the synagogue.

So I remained here to rock the baby to sleep and to watch over him."

WORTHY JEWS

As the recital of the awe-inspiring *Kol Nidrei* ushering in Yom Kippur was about to begin, Rabbi Levi Isaac of Berditchev took a lighted candle in one hand, got down on his knees and searched under the benches. Asked what he was looking for, the rabbi replied: "Jews." Standing erect, he lifted his eyes to heaven, saying:

"Master of the Universe! See what a wonderful people are the Jews! Today, the eve of the Day of Atonement, when it is considered meritorious for a Jew to eat and drink more than usual, there is not even one drunk nor anyone sick from overeating lying under the benches. Are not Your children really good? Are they not worthy of being inscribed and sealed for a year of health, happiness and prosperity?"

NO CAUSE FOR WORRY

As the *Kol Nidrei* service was about to start, the rabbi, noticing that a trustee standing next to him had suddenly turned pale, solicitously whispered to him:

"Are you ill?"

"No," the trustee softly yet nervously replied. "However, I just reminded myself that I forgot to lock the door of my house when I left for the synagogue."

"Don't worry," the rabbi reassuringly said. "I have observed that all of the other trustees are already in the synagogue."

The Day of Atonement

Even though the Day of Atonement is the culmination of the penitential days, the rabbis have taught that "the Israelites never had such joyous holidays as . . . Yom Kippur" (Taanit 30b). On this fast day, mourning is prohibited and white clothes are worn as a symbol of purity and festivity. To avert a severe decree on this judgment day, penitence, prayer and charity must be practiced. Hence, petitions for forgiveness constitute a major portion of the prayer ritual of the day and the duty to perform charity and good deeds is stressed.

FRIENDLY ENEMIES

Berel and Shmerel, friendly enemies, were constantly engaged in petty quarrels, more often than not spiced with sharp expletives and harsh curses. One year on the eve of Yom Kippur, when it is customary to ask forgiveness from both friend and foe, Berel approached Shmerel in the synagogue and said to him in a tone of appeasement:

"As good Jews, let's agree before the Day of Atonement to cease quarreling."

Shmerel, in a solemn mood of repentance, promptly acquiesced:

"I agree with you. I'll pray also that the Almighty grant you all that you ask Him for me."

"Shame on you!" Berel angrily cried. "Even on the eve of Yom Kippur in the synagogue you still harbor wicked thoughts about me."

Opening the Gates of Repentance

A young, illiterate herdsman who dwelt in isolation throughout the year came to the synagogue of the Baal Shem Tov, the founder of the Hasidic movement, on the Day of Atonement. Although the lad was unable to join the congregation in prayer, he grasped the significance and spirit of the occasion as the day wore on. He experienced a strong, urgent emotion to participate with the congregation in pleading for atonement. As the *Neilah* service was drawing to a close, the herdsman removed from his pocket a reed whistle that he used while tending his flock and blew on it lustily.

Hearing the solemn sanctity of the *Neilah* prayers disturbed, the *Hasidim* angrily scolded the lad. However, the Baal Shem Tov in a calm, decisive voice, took his followers to task:

"Despite all your prayers, your learning and your piety, you haven't learned to repent and you haven't been able to prevail upon God to grant you pardon. This illiterate young herdsman, possessed with a sincere desire to serve the Almighty, has opened the gates of repentance for all of us."

A Lenient Illiterate

Levi Isaac of Berditchev once asked an illiterate Jew what he did on Yom Kippur since he could not read the prescribed prayers.

The Jew reluctantly replied:

"I spoke to God and told Him that the sins for which I'm supposed to repent are really minor ones. I also said to Him: 'My sins are inconsequential but Yours are really grave. You have removed mothers from their children and children from their mothers. So let's reach an agreement. If You'll pardon me, I'm ready to pardon You.' "

The Berditchever rabbi angrily rebuked the unlettered Jew:

"You are not only illiterate but you are also foolish. You were too lenient with God. You should have insisted that He bring redemption to the entire Jewish people."

FORGIVENESS FOR TRUTH-TELLING

Appealing to God for forgiveness, Rabbi Levi Isaac prayed as follows:

"Once Jews lied to You when on the Day of Atonement they intoned: 'We have sinned, we have dealt treacherously, we have robbed, we have spoken slander . . .' In truth, they never sinned, nor did they deal treacherously, nor did they rob, nor did they speak slander. We, however, have committed all of these sins and we are telling You the truth. For our truthfulness, You must forgive us."

REDEMPTION FOR THE WORLD

The Berditchever rabbi ascended the pulpit before *Neilah* and addressed the congregation:

"Our sages have taught that whoever quotes a passage in the name of the one who said it brings redemption to the world. Therefore I say: 'And God said: I have pardoned according to your words.' "

A GOOD REASON TO SIN

A rabbi, enthralled with the beautiful and stirring singing of "O, pardon us" by the sweet-voiced cantor, raised his eyes on high and asked:

"Master of the Universe, answer my question: If the children of Israel would not sin, who would chant so beautifully 'O, pardon us'?"

HEART BEATS

Rabbi Israel Meir, famed as the author of *Hafetz Hayyim,* was expounding the customs of Yom Kippur. Referring to the practice of beating one's heart when the confession of sins is recited, he explained:

"God does not forgive the sins of one who smites his heart but he pardons those whose hearts smite them."

SPEAK FOR YOURSELF

On the eve of Yom Kippur a Jew appeared before Rabbi Naphtali Tzvi Horowitz of Ropshitz to confess and make atonement for his sins in accordance with whatever penance the rabbi might impose upon him. Ashamed of the multitude of his unlawful commissions, he said to the rabbi:

"A friend of mine who is guilty of many sins requested me to ask you for the proper method of atoning before Yom Kippur. He failed to attend the synagogue regularly. He even missed his private devotions occasionally. Once he violated the Sabbath by transacting business."

Rabbi Naphtali, undeceived, said:

"Your friend is most foolish. He could have come to me and pretended that a friend sent him."

EVEN ONE IS TOO MUCH

On the Day of Atonement, a humble, pious Jew interrupted the prescribed order of prayers at the recital of the lengthy detailing of sins and interjected his own plea:

"Heavenly Father, why do you hold the Jewish people responsible for so many sins? No people has endured the trials and tribulations that have been the fate of the Jews. They have suffered a long and bitter exile. Therefore, I believe that Israel is indeed a holy people for it is a wonder that they obey even one of Your commandments."

A YOM KIPPUR FRUSTRATION

One of the guests at Grossinger's, the famed resort hotel, confided this story: One Yom Kippur he attended the services at Grossinger's. He looked out the window of the temple and saw the sunlit fairway. The temptation was too strong. He walked out of the services, went over to the clubhouse, took his clubs and began to play.

On the short 3rd hole he fulfilled his life's ambition and scored a hole-in-one.

"I know what you're going to say," he sighed. "That I was punished. Well, I was. Because it was Yom Kippur nobody saw me make it. And because it was Yom Kippur I couldn't tell anybody about it."

TREMBLING FISH

Why is it said that on the awe-inspiring Day of Atonement even the fish in the waters tremble?

The explanation is simple. When Jews observe *Tashlich* on the New Year by casting their sins into the waters, the fish swallow them. Is it a wonder that the fish, burdened with so many sins, tremble with fear on the Day of Atonement?

TRUTH AND FALSEHOOD

Congregation Anshei Sheker was evidently unable to engage a suitable rabbi for it was habitually changing its spiritual leaders.

The latest rabbi quickly felt the pulse of the congregation and made up his mind that he too would not remain long. He devoted the Yom Kippur sermon to the subject of truth, complimenting the congregation on their abhorrence of falsehood and their love of truth.

During an intermission before the afternoon service, the president congratulated the rabbi on the excellent message he had delivered. He added:

"You are the first rabbi that ever spoke kindly to our congregation. I hope you are sincere."

"I meant every word I said," the rabbi assured him. "You know that today when we recite the confession of sins we ask forgiveness 'for the sin which we have committed before Thee by despising parents and teachers.' The members of our congregation are apparently unwilling to tell a falsehood on Yom Kippur so they make certain to spurn their teachers."

A Greater Crime

Two neighboring rabbis met on the eve of Yom Kippur. One was known for his leniency in the interpretation of Jewish law while the other had the reputation of adhering strictly to the minutiae of every tradition and custom. The former said to the latter:

"Please forgive me if I tell you that you require much more divine mercy than I need. We know that the Day of Atonement brings pardon for sins committed against God but not for crimes perpetrated upon a person. If I erred in interpreting a law by permitting something that is actually forbidden, then I violated God's law and Yom Kippur will bring me atonement. If you were wrong in rendering a decision and forbade the use of something that is permissible, then you are guilty of causing a loss to a Jew which will not be forgiven on Yom Kippur."

A Fifty-Fifty Proposition

To earn an honest livelihood, Ephraim Greidiger, the famous wit, sold candles. One day he arrived in the town of Helm, noted for its "wise men," and was deeply disappointed for no one bought any candles. It didn't take Ephraim long to devise a new sales approach. Standing in the main street of Helm, he proclaimed in a loud voice:

"Tomorrow is the Day of Atonement! Buy memorial candles!"

In no time at all, Ephraim's entire stock was sold out.

Then the "wise men" of Helm, greatly perturbed, approached Ephraim and said:

"If tomorrow is the Day of Atonement, we must pray for atonement. What can we do if there isn't among us a cantor to conduct the service?"

The wit assured them that he was quite capable of being the "Messenger of the Congregation" if he would be properly remunerated. They readily agreed to pay him ten rubles for his services.

Rejoicing that the candle peddler had arrived in Helm in time to remind them of the holiest day of the year, the townsmen assembled in the synagogue towards evening for the services.

As the self-styled cantor led the congregation in the Yom Kippur evening service, Manasseh, a neighbor of Ephraim, arrived in Helm. Manasseh, amazed to find all the shops closed and the streets empty on an ordinary weekday evening, wended his way to the synagogue.

As Manasseh entered the synagogue and stood aghast at the rear, Ephraim, facing the congregation, recognized his fellow townsman. Fearing lest Manasseh spoil his business, Ephraim raised his voice and chanted in Hebrew to the melody of one of the traditional prayers:

"Peace unto you, my neighbor." He continued singing the entire episode of his arrival in Helm, his business failure, the method he devised to sell his candles, and, finally, how he was engaged as the cantor. Concluding his recital, he chanted in a penitent and pleading tone as befitted the Day of Atonement:

"If you will not divulge my plot, I will give you half of the ten rubles I am earning."

From the rear of the synagogue was heard the loud, clear voice of Manasseh responding with the proper intonation:

"Amen."

A Fearful Cantor

Although he had no experience as a cantor, a pious *Hasid* was invited by his rabbi to be the Messenger of the Congregation on Yom Kippur. He approached the divine leader as the *Kol Nidrei* service was about to start and said:

"Rabbi, I am possessed with fear."

The rabbi reassured him:

"Precisely for the reason that you have the fear of God I want you to lead the services."

A Unique Prayer

An orphaned Jewish boy, reared by a Christian family, never had an opportunity to learn the ways of his forebears although he did know at least that he was Jewish. He had inherited from his father a Hebrew prayer book which he cherished dearly. When the lad was about seven years old, he was invited by the sexton of the local synagogue to attend the services on the Day of Atonement. The youngster cheerfully accepted the invitation and came to the synagogue with his prayer book.

The boy felt very uncomfortable because he was unable to join the congregation in prayer. In desperation, he shouted:

"Lord! Listen to me also. I was never taught how to

pray and I don't know what to tell you; however, I have my father's prayer book with me. Take it—I give you the entire book."

SILENT DEVOTION

On Yom Kippur, an eight-year-old boy, seated next to his father in the synagogue, was reading the prayers inaudibly. His father gently whispered to him:

"Son, I can't hear you praying."

"I wasn't talking to you," the boy replied in a firm tone.

A FERVENT PLEA

Motke, reputed to be a petty thief, joined the congregation on the Day of Atonement and was observed praying quite devoutly. Knowing that Motke was unable to read the prayers, the sexton drew near him to overhear what he was saying. Indeed, Motke's prayer was original and he uttered it with much feeling:

"O, Lord our God! Protect me from doing evil. Guard me and all the Jews from thievery. However, if You do decree that there should be thefts, please let me be the one to handle them."

WHY AN ATHEIST PRAYS

A free-thinker, observed praying fervently during the Yom Kippur services, was asked the reason for his sudden piety. He sheepishly explained:

"You know that I am an atheist. However, as an unbeliever, I also have doubts about atheism."

PRAYER FORBIDDEN

A young man was anxious to visit his elderly mother in the synagogue on Yom Kippur to see how she was faring on the fast day. Coming to the synagogue, he found the entrance blocked by a uniformed guard who demanded that he produce a ticket for a seat. He explained that he did not intend to remain in the synagogue but that he only wanted to see his mother for a few minutes.

The Irish guard was indeed sympathetic but he had no authorization to allow anyone without a ticket to enter the house of worship. He thoughtfully considered how he might grant the young man's request without violating his duty. Finally, he said:

"O.K. You can go in to see your mother but God help you if I catch you praying."

THE DUTY OF A SOLDIER

After the evening service of Yom Kippur, Rabbi Joseph Dov Ber Soloveitchik of Brisk observed that a wealthy member of his congregation was remaining in the synagogue to recite Psalms. The sage said to him reproachingly:

"Every soldier in an army is assigned to a division—artillery, cavalry or infantry. Naturally, he has no authority to change from one division to another. If he does change without permission of the proper authorities, he has to face court-martial.

"Every Jew is a soldier in the army of the Lord and is given an assignment which he cannot change without authorization. The recital of Psalms is the assignment given to the poor for repentance on the Day of Atonement. However, you, as a wealthy person, have been assigned the giving of charity to fulfill your responsibility for repentance. If you don't want to be court-martialed by the Court on High, you had better fulfill your assignment."

Eating on Yom Kippur

It is true that eating on the Day of Atonement is permitted—under certain circumstances. Curious and odd are a number of incidents that occurred where people broke the fast, usually outside of the law. More significant is the tendency of rabbis towards leniency in the case of the ill.

LENIENCY IN SEVERITY

Rabbi Hayyim Soloveitchik of Brisk of the past century was asked why he was so lenient in permitting sick people to eat on the Day of Atonement. He replied subtly:

"I am not lenient. On the contrary, I am very severe when it comes to saving lives."

A LESSON IN SELF-SACRIFICE

A rabbi summoned before him a Jew who had been seen eating on Yom Kippur. In response to the rabbi's harsh words of censure, the sinner apologetically confessed:

"I am aware of my grave sin but I committed an act

of self-sacrifice. I violated the day of fasting to help a needy Jewish girl."

"Aiding a poor girl is indeed noteworthy," agreed the rabbi. "However, I still do not understand why it was necessary for you to eat."

The sinner amplified his explanation:

"On the morning of Yom Kippur, while on the way to the synagogue, I overheard two girls conversing. One said to the other: 'I wish I would have a hundred dollars for every Jew who will eat today.' I immediately decided to pray that her wish would come true and, to help her further with an additional hundred dollars, I ate."

CONFESSION OF A MINOR SIN

On the eve of the Day of Atonement a Jew came to his rabbi to confess a sin.

"What was the sin you committed?" the rabbi asked.

"It happened once that I didn't recite the grace after meals."

"Why not?"

"Because I didn't say the benediction for bread before I ate."

"Why not?"

"Because I didn't wash my hands before the meal."

"Why not?"

"Because there was no place in the restaurant for washing hands."

"Is it possible that in a *Kosher* restaurant there wouldn't be facilities for washing hands?"

"But it wasn't a *Kosher* restaurant."

"How did you dare to eat in a non-*Kosher* restaurant?"

"I didn't have any choice. All the *Kosher* restaurants were closed."

"How did it happen that all the *Kosher* restaurants were closed?"

"It was Yom Kippur."

DRINKING PERMITTED

On the afternoon of the Day of Atonement, Baruch, pale-faced and glassy-eyed, approached the rabbi and pleaded in a weak voice:

"I don't feel well, rabbi. I am parched and I can't stand the thirst."

The rabbi, seeing the appearance of Baruch, became panicky and feared that if he did not permit his congregant to drink he might become critically sick.

"Since it's apparent that you may endanger your life if you don't quench your thirst, I permit you to have a glass of water," the rabbi decreed.

"You are most generous, rabbi. For your kindness I promise you that never again will I eat herring for breakfast on Yom Kippur."

A QUICK THIRST QUENCHER

During the Day of Atonement, the sexton told the rabbi that a congregant had fainted due to the fast and asked if he could give him some water.

"Give him a spoonful of water," the rabbi said.

A few minutes later the sexton reported to the rabbi that the man was revived but had asked for more water.

This time the sage decreed differently:

"Tell him that he can drink as much water as he requires provided he donates a dollar to the synagogue for each spoonful of water."

As soon as the rabbi's ruling was told to the revived congregant, his thirst suddenly disappeared and he felt sufficiently refreshed to continue with the Yom Kippur prayers.

A Secret Practice Revealed

An old Jew, having dwelt all his life on a farm remote from other Jews, came to spend his last years in a Jewish community. Although he enjoyed the synagogue services, many of the customs were unfamiliar to him. During the first Yom Kippur he observed with a congregation, he asked a new acquaintance what one does when he wraps the *Talis* over his head and kneels on the floor. The acquaintance said:

"There is a secret practice of the Jews which I will reveal to you provided you do not repeat it to a soul. Every Jew hides bread in his *Talis* and, when he kneels on the floor with his head completely covered, he eats it."

The following year on the Day of Atonement as the congregation rose after kneeling, they noticed that the old man was still down on his knees. A neighbor nudged him and said quietly:

"Get up. We've finished."

The old man turned up his face and said:

"Why do you begrudge me? You have teeth so that you can eat quickly but I am toothless and it takes me longer to chew."

Eating Permitted for the Ill

The rabbi, having learned that Yossel Luksh had eaten on the Day of Atonement, summoned the culprit and rebuked him:

"It is a grave sin to eat on Yom Kippur!"

"I was taught, rabbi, that if one is ill he is permitted to eat," Yossel explained.

"Only if one is critically ill may he eat. Were you so seriously ill?"

"Rabbi, you should be ashamed of yourself," declared Yossel. "You admit that I may eat but first you want me to become very sick. I am amazed that you begrudge me my health."

"Wipe Off Your Lips!"

Joe and Max met on the afternoon of Yom Kippur.

Joe: I assume you are fasting today.

Max: Certainly. Why do you even ask?

Joe: You should wipe off your lips.

Max, hastening to obey: It was foolish of me not to have wiped my lips before.

Joe, grinning impishly: There was nothing on your lips. I was only fooling.

A Short Day of Atonement

An American Jew bemoaned the recent death of Rabbi Jacob Hammer, former spiritual leader in Finland.

"I will miss Rabbi Hammer when the Day of Atonement comes," he told a friend. "Because of him I was obliged to fast only half a day last Yom Kippur."

The friend, incredulous, remarked:

"I can't imagine that the pious rabbi, may his soul rest in peace, permitted you to eat on Yom Kippur."

"Not only did he allow me to eat but he also ate with me," the Jew retorted.

"How is that possible?"

"Rabbi Hammer was an expert in the calendar. He figured out that in Finland the day of Yom Kippur was over when it was noon here."

THE FEAR OF DEATH

Reuben Asher Braudes was critically ill. On the eve of the Day of Atonement some of his friends gathered at his bedside. Suddenly he burst forth into tears.

"Why are you crying, Reuben?" he was asked. "Do you perchance fear the Day of Judgment?"

"Not at all," the stalwart unbeliever responded. "I am afraid that I might die today and then I will be forced to fast tomorrow."

LOOKING AHEAD

Looking through a window of the synagogue on the Day of Atonement, a father was appalled to see his son engaged in an intimate chat with a beautiful girl. When the boy returned to his seat, the parent spoke angrily to him:

"I'm ashamed of you! How dare you engage in a frivolous conversation with a girl on this day of prayer and fasting?"

"Don't worry, Dad," the boy responded. "I was just making a date with her for Simhas Torah."

NEXT YEAR IN SYNAGOGUE AGAIN

As the congregants were rushing pell-mell to depart from the synagogue at the conclusion of the *Neilah* service, the sexton gave a loud bang with his hand on the reading table to attract attention. When some semblance of order was achieved, the sexton shouted above the hubbub:

"*Kol Nidrei* services for the coming Yom Kippur will begin at six p.m."

The young rabbi hastened to the sexton and asked:

"Why didn't you announce the time for the coming Friday evening services?"

"You should know, rabbi," the experienced sexton replied, "that these Jews won't be seen again in the synagogue until next Yom Kippur."

SATAN THE ACCUSER

How is it known that Satan cannot act as an accuser on Yom Kippur? Rama bar Hama said: The total of the numerical equivalents of the Hebrew letters in *HaSaTaN* is 364. Therefore it is deduced that only on 364 days Satan may act as an accuser, but on Yom Kippur he is not permitted to do so.

FOLK PROVERBS

When one blows, it becomes cold. (From the New Moon of Elul, when the blowing of the Shofar begins, autumn arrives.)

Crooked as a Shofar!

A whole year she was idle but on the eve of Yom Kippur she began many things.

On the eve of Yom Kippur, thieves become pious.

A man sins and an innocent chicken becomes the atonement.

SUKKOS—FESTIVAL OF BOOTHS

Preparing for the Festival

CHAPTER FOUR

SUKKOS—THE FESTIVAL OF BOOTHS

*T*HE *Bible records at length the origin and significance of Sukkos, the longest and most joyous of the Jewish festivals. "And the Lord spoke unto Moses, saying: Speak unto the children of Israel, saying: "On the fifteenth day of this seventh month is the feast of tabernacles for seven days unto the Lord . . . on the eighth day shall be a holy convocation unto you . . . it is a day of solemn assembly . . . Howbeit on the fifteenth day of the seventh month, when ye have gathered in the fruits of the land, ye shall keep the feast of the Lord seven days; on the first day shall be a solemn rest, and on the eighth day shall be a solemn rest. And ye shall take you on the first day the fruit of goodly trees, branches of palm-trees, and boughs of thick trees, and willows of the brook, and ye shall rejoice before the Lord your God seven days. And ye shall keep it a feast unto the Lord seven days in the year . . . Ye shall dwell in booths seven days; all that are home-born in Israel shall dwell in booths; that your generations may know that I made the children of Israel to dwell in booths, when I brought them out of the land of Egypt . . ." (Leviticus 23.33–43).*

113

The eight days of the Festival of Booths, including Shemini Atzeres, the Eighth Day of Solemn Assembly, are called in the liturgy "the Season of Our Rejoicing," and then the period is concluded with Simhas Torah, the Festival of the Rejoicing in the Law. It is a season of joyous thanksgiving for the bounties of the Almighty. It is at the same time a reminder that good fortune and gladness need to be shared with the unfortunate and the stranger. Tales of the Hasidic rabbis reflect the spiritual and material generosity associated with this festival.

A Promise Redeemed

The Jews of Berditchev were sorely distressed for there was no *Esrog* available for Sukkos. To solve the problem, Rabbi Levi Isaac dispatched a messenger to purchase at least one *Esrog* regardless of the cost. On the outskirts of Berditchev, the messenger encountered a Jew carrying a beautiful *Esrog* and escorted him to Rabbi Levi Isaac. The rabbi tried in every imaginable way to persuade the *Esrog* owner to remain in Berditchev over the festival so that the entire community could pronounce the benediction over his *Esrog,* but the man was adamant. He had to be on his way.

Finally, Rabbi Levi Isaac made the man this proposal: "If you will remain in Berditchev for Sukkos, I promise that you will share with me my portion in the future world."

Upon hearing this promise of the righteous rabbi, the Jew readily acquiesced and brought joy to the Jews of Berditchev.

Later, the rabbi told his sexton to advise the Berditchever Jews not to let the stranger enter any *Sukkah* in the town.

On the first day of Sukkos the Jew wanted to enter the *Sukkah* of the inn where he was lodging but, to his utter amazement, he was refused admittance. He tried several other nearby booths where he faced the identical fate. Realizing that there was undoubtedly a plot against him, he ran in desperation to the rabbi and bitterly cried:

"Have I sinned? Haven't I allowed you to use my *Esrog?* Why don't you permit me to fulfill the commandment of dwelling in a *Sukkah?*"

Rabbi Levi Isaac replied:

"If you will release me from my promise concerning the future world, I will arrange that you be permitted to enter any *Sukkah* in Berditchev."

The stranger reflected on the choices confronting him. On the one hand, it was no light matter to renounce the privilege of sharing the future world with such a pious and learned man as Rabbi Levi Isaac; on the other hand, it was inconceivable that he should disregard the commandment of dwelling in the *Sukkah*. The latter consideration weighed heavily in his mind and he accepted the rabbi's ultimatum.

At the conclusion of the festival, Rabbi Levi Isaac summoned the stranger and said to him:

"I herewith restore my promise to you. I want you to know that I was reluctant for you to earn a share of my portion in Eternal Life through bartering. However, now that you have been tempted to violate God's commandment and you have bravely withstood the temptation, you truly merit my original promise."

Requisites for Sukkos

The Dzikover rabbi was beseeched by one of his *Hasidim* that he be given a special benediction to be assured of obtaining a stately palm branch, a perfect *Esrog* and beautiful myrtle twigs and willows of the brook for the observance of Sukkos. The rabbi forthrightly answered him:

"What you require for Sukkos is an honest mind, a generous heart and a meek spirit. When you will have acquired these possessions, then you can seek to obtain an extraordinary *Esrog* and *Lulav*."

A Negligible Duty

On the eve of Sukkos, it was a custom of the famous Rabbi Hayyim Halberstam of Sandz to spend the day dispensing charity. To meet the needs of the many indigent persons who sought his assistance, he would borrow money from the *Esrogim* merchants who had cash at that time.

Once his son said to him:

"Father, you were unable to buy a beautiful *Esrog* and *Lulav* and our *Sukkah* is smaller than usual yet you are giving away borrowed money. I know that charity is an important duty but there is no place where it is written that a person is obligated to borrow money to be charitable."

The father angrily chided his offspring:

"How can you say such a thing? What would you have me do? You know that I do not have knowledge of the Torah nor fear of God. I can only dispense charity and you would want me to sacrifice even that small duty."

No School on Sukkos

A five-year-old, tear-faced girl who stood in front of her home was asked by a neighbor:

"Darling, why do you look so sad?"

"Tomorrow is Sukkos and my brother will have a holiday from school," the girl replied in a tone of deep anguish.

"Won't you also have a holiday?" the friendly neighbor asked.

"No," wept the child. "I haven't started to go to school yet."

In the Sukkah

The Sukkah is a reminder of the booths in which the children of Israel lived during their wanderings in the wilderness after their redemption from Egyptian slavery. Pious Jews not only eat but also dwell in the Sukkah during the entire festival so that they might faithfully commemorate the historic event that it symbolizes. As living in a booth is not usually comfortable, women, minors and the sick are exempt from this duty. However, guests are always welcome. Indeed, a special prayer of welcome to guests—Ushpizin—is recited as one enters the Sukkah. This Aramaic prayer extends a hospitable invitation to the holy guests

*—Abraham, Isaac, Jacob, Joseph, Moses, Aaron
and David. As these sainted persons would undoubtedly refuse to dwell in a Sukkah where
poor persons are not welcome, it is customary
to invite indigent persons to dine and drink
and enjoy the festival. As a matter of fact, the
temporary and frail Sukkah recalls the uncertainty of life and the hardships of the poor.
The exemption of women from the Sukkah
and the welcome to the needy are the subject
of some interesting anecdotes.*

HOSPITALITY IN THE SUKKAH

Every year Rabbi Levi Isaac of Berditchev invited
many simpletons and ignoramuses to his *Sukkah.* When
he was asked why he saw fit to extend hospitality to
such people, the sage replied:

"In the future world, where the righteous will dwell
in the Tabernacle of Eternal Peace, I will also want
to be among them. I fear that I will not be permitted
to enter the Tabernacle for it is not seemly that such
a lowly person as myself can be on the same level as
the righteous. Therefore, I am establishing a just
claim for myself. If the angels will ask me: 'How can
you, an ignorant man, expect to be admitted into the
Sukkah of Peace,' I will be able to reply to them: 'I
welcomed simple people into my *Sukkah.*'"

"COME INTO MY SUKKAH!"

On the eve of Sukkos, a carpenter, attired in work
clothes and with his tools slung over his back, was

wending his way through a forest, homeward bound
to observe the festival. To his great distress, he lost
his way and wandered aimlessly. When darkness fell,
he saw lights burning in a small dwelling not far ahead.
Approaching cautiously, he opened the door slightly
and peeked in.

In the room he saw a rabbi and a group of *Hasidim*
clothed in festive garments and seated in a beautifully
decorated *Sukkah,* partaking of a sumptuous repast.
Ashamed of his appearance, the carpenter was on the
verge of leaving, when the rabbi, in a cordial tone,
called to him:

"What are you staring at? Is it beneath your dignity
to sit in my *Sukkah?* Come into my *Sukkah* and join
us!"

The Result of Dwelling in a Sukkah

On the festival of Sukkos, an extremely pious Jew
was not feeling too well. Despite the warning of his
wife that he might catch a cold if he slept in the *Sukkah,*
he spent most of the holiday in the booth in accordance
with Jewish tradition. As his wife foresaw, he caught
a cold which developed into pneumonia.

The spouse self-righteously chided her husband:

"See what happened to you because you slept in
the *Sukkah."*

"You have a woman's understanding," he retorted.
"It's true that I'm ill because I fulfilled the commandment of dwelling in a *Sukkah.* However, can you imagine how severe my illness would have been if I hadn't
done my duty?"

How Man Can Rejoice on a Festival

A shrewish woman angrily remonstrated with her husband Hershel:

"You told me that the Torah says about Sukkos 'And ye shall rejoice in your festival.' Why then are women exempt from the *Mitzvah* of sitting in the *Sukkah* and only men enjoy this privilege?"

Hershel arose, running to the door, and said over his shoulder:

"The Torah understands that a man can rejoice on the festival only if he is without his wife."

Woman's Exemption from the Sukkah

Why are women exempt from dwelling in the *Sukkah?*

Man never receives two punishments simultaneously. To dwell in a *Sukkah* is a punishment in itself. To have one's wife in a *Sukkah* would be an additional punishment.

A Harsh Decree

A government official visiting a Jewish town in Galicia on the first day of Sukkos was amazed to see the large number of booths erected by the Jews for the celebration of the festival. He commanded the mayor of the town:

"Issue immediately an order to the Jews to destroy these booths for they have undoubtedly been built without government sanction."

Without delay, the mayor, a friend of the Jews who knew their traditions, issued the following decree:

"Attention all Jews! You are hereby notified that all booths must be destroyed within ten days. Failure to fulfill this order will result in severe punishment."

RENTAL FOR A SUKKAH

Berel and Shmerel reached an agreement whereby Berel would construct a *Sukkah* in his backyard and Shmerel would pay rent for using it during the festival of Sukkos. After the holiday Berel claimed the rental fee that had been stipulated. Shocked when Shmerel refused to fulfill his agreement, Berel summoned him for a hearing before the local rabbi.

When the rabbi heard Berel's story, he decreed that Shmerel need not pay anything.

Both the plaintiff and the defendant were equally astonished at this judicial decision. Seeing the amazement that covered their faces, the rabbi explained:

"The Talmud says that the obligation to dwell in a *Sukkah* should be fulfilled in the same manner as one dwells in his house. Last week you, Shmerel, appeared before me on the complaint of your landlord. If you do not pay rent for your house, why should you pay rent for the *Sukkah?*"

The Esrog

The festival of Sukkos is truly rich in symbols. Besides dwelling in the Sukkah, the Jew takes four species so that he "shall rejoice before the Lord" with them. The species are: Esrog, the fragrant citron; Lulav, the stately palm branch; the myrtle branch and the wil-

lows of the brook. An ordinary Esrog is usually not considered suitable and no expense is spared in the acquisition of the choicest citron. Because of the high cost, Esrogim are frequently bought in partnership as it is considered meritorious to own one, even if only partially. An Esrog needs to be flawless, beautiful, perfect, whole in every respect. Its Pitma, the pestle-like protuberance, must not become detached. As the Esrogim of Corfu were renowned for their beauty, it is no wonder that this proverb was current among East European Jews: "A girl like a Corfu Esrog!"

CHOOSING ESROGIM

It was a custom in Slonim that before a Jew bought an *Esrog* he would bring it to Rabbi Eizel Harif for an opinion as to its suitability for use. One year the rabbi was dissatisfied with the entire crop of *Esrogim* that were being sold. As each Jew came with the *Esrog* he had selected to purchase, the rabbi refused to give his stamp of approval.

When the *Esrogim* dealer became aware of what was happening, he hastened to the rabbi and complained bitterly:

"What are you doing to me, rabbi? No one is buying an *Esrog* and I'll suffer a great financial loss. I depend for a livelihood upon the sale of *Esrogim*. Because of your advice, I'll not have the means to support my family during the coming year."

The rabbi, sincerely distraught that he might be the cause of a human's suffering, told the dealer:

"It's a fact that your *Esrogim* are unsuitable and, when my judgment is asked, I must tell the truth. God forbid, however, that I should cause a Jew to suffer. I'll tell you what to do. Give every prospective buyer two *Esrogim* instead of one. As he will ask me which one of the two *Esrogim* is better, I'll then be able to answer truthfully that one is better than the other and your sales will be assured."

A RARE PRIVILEGE

Although Rabbi Mordecai of Neschiz was a pauper, he saved money regularly by stinting himself just so that he would have enough to purchase an extraordinary *Esrog*. The week before the holiday he went to Brody with his frugally hoarded money. Entering the town, he encountered a coachman, weeping copiously alongside a dead horse.

Rabbi Mordecai inquired sympathetically:

"Why are you so dejected?"

"My horse was just killed in an accident. Without a horse I can't earn a living."

The rabbi was not slow in responding. Handing his *Esrog* money to the coachman, he told him to use it to purchase another horse. Thereupon, Rabbi Mordecai returned to Neschiz, arriving in a mood of exhilaration. Many of his townsmen gathered about him and asked to see his *Esrog*.

"All Jews will pronounce the benediction over the *Esrog* during Sukkos," Rabbi Mordecai blandly informed the curiosity seekers. "Only I have been granted the rare privilege to recite the blessing over a horse."

No Blessing Required

Reb Yoseph, a rich and pious householder, was most meticulous in the fulfillment of all the commandments of the Torah. He was especially particular about a proper *Esrog* for Sukkos and no price was too high for him to secure the best that was available.

On the first day of the festival, he arose early to perform the duty of reciting the blessing over the *Esrog*.

Reb Yoseph's servant had the same idea and he arose even earlier. Taking the *Esrog* from its silver case, the servant began to recite the preliminary prayer *Yehi Ratzon*. Suddenly, he was surprised and shocked to hear the approaching footsteps of Reb Yoseph. His hands trembled and the *Esrog* fell to the floor. Looking down, he was further distressed to see that the *Pitma* was broken off. At that moment, Reb Yoseph entered the room and observed the pale, frightened face of his servant staring at the now unfit *Esrog*.

Reb Yoseph, his own face wreathed in kindness, gently said;

"If the *Esrog* is unsuitable for use, the blessing need not be said."

The Lot of a Beautiful Esrog

Reluctant to function in the active rabbinate, Rabbi Jacob Koslover declined an invitation to serve as the rabbi of Brezshan. His wife, however, anxious to be the *Rebbetzin* of such an important Jewish community, kept urging him to reconsider.

During the week preceding Sukkos, the *Rebbetzin*

was nagging him more than usual. Finally, Rabbi
Jacob said to her:

"If you will buy a beautiful *Esrog* for me, I will reconsider the offer."

The wife hastened to the marketplace and selected
the choicest *Esrog* for which she gladly paid an ex-
orbitant price.

Learning of his exceptional *Esrog*, many Jews flocked
to his home on the first day of Sukkos to pronounce the
blessing over it. Before the day was done, the *Esrog*
became black and spotted and lost its beautiful appearance.

Pointing to the now unseemly *Esrog*, Rabbi Jacob
said to his wife:

"You can now see that even the most exquisite *Esrog*
becomes spoiled when it falls into communal hands."

"THIS ESROG IS AN ESROG"

The "wise men" of Helm rejoiced exceedingly over
the *Esrog* that the president of their congregation had
purchased for Sukkos. This was not just an ordinary
Esrog. It came from the Land of Israel. It was yellow
as the color of an *Esrog*. It was fragrant as the odor of
an *Esrog*. It was without a blemish as an *Esrog*. It had
a *Pitma* that was firm and stately. In short, this was an
Esrog!

The president of the congregation reluctantly gave
the *Esrog* to the sexton to take it to all of the Helm
householders so that they could recite the traditional
blessing over it. Fearful of the sexton's carelessness, the
president warned him:

"Remember! This *Esrog* is *an Esrog!* Handle with extreme care. Be especially cautious that the *Pitma* should not be spoiled by handling for if this should happen the *Esrog* will be unsuitable for use. Remember! This *Esrog* is *an Esrog.*"

The wise sexton joyfully embarked on his holy mission. Firmly clutching the *Esrog* in both hands, he started out through the streets of Helm. A sudden inspiration caused him to stop dead in his tracks. He looked at the *Esrog* in his hands. He held it level with his eyes. He stared intently at it. He scrutinized the *Esrog* from all sides. Shutting his eyes tightly, the sexton devoutly meditated, recalling in detail the instructions of the president. He fully realized the necessity to take extreme precautions that the *Pitma* should not be spoiled. His own keen insight confirmed the president's warning. Ah, he was shrewd! But what was the inspiration that brought him to a sudden halt? Had he forgotten his clever device? No! No! He knew what he had to do. No sooner said than done!

Taking a sharp knife from his pocket, the scrupulous sexton carefully cut the *Pitma* from the *Esrog.* Of course, he would not throw the *Pitma* away. The president had ordered him to take good care of it. He would never dare disobey the president. So the sexton took the *Pitma* and wrapped it in a clean handkerchief which he gently placed in his pocket. He then proceeded with the *Esrog* to the homes of the "wise Helmites" to allow them the privilege of reciting the blessing over the *Esrog.*

As the sexton entered each home, he reiterated the president's caution:

"Remember! This *Esrog* is *an Esrog!*"

An Esrog in Partnership

Before Sukkos a peddler went from house to house in Helm selling *Esrogim*. A wise Helmite regretfully told the peddler that, although he was most anxious to have an *Esrog*, he could afford only half the price that was asked. The peddler received the same response in the next house. He brought the two neighbors together and suggested to them that if each would pay half the price of the *Esrog* they could buy it in partnership. This economical proposal appealed to the neighboring Helmites and they paid the peddler for the *Esrog*. The latter thanked them profusely and continued on his way.

Not long after, the two neighbors began to quarrel over who should use the *Esrog* first. Unable to reach a decision, the feuding men appeared before the elders of the Helm community to seek justice. There was no precedent, however, to guide the elders in reaching a decision, and they deliberated for seven days and seven nights before the problem was finally solved to everyone's satisfaction. The solution was this: The *Esrog* was to be cut in equal halves so that each one would receive the share for which he had paid.

A Conscientious Miser

The Jews of a small town decided to share the cost of an *Esrog* and a *Lulav*. Only Kamtzan, the local miser, refused to contribute his share. On the first day of Sukkos, when the sexton was carrying the *Esrog* and *Lulav* from house to house so that all could pronounce the special benediction, he naturally skipped the house of Kamtzan. The miser, however, was hiding near a neighbor's house. As the sexton came along, Kamtzan grabbed him from behind and lifted him into the air. Holding the sexton aloft, Kamtzan waved him heavenwards, earthwards and to the four winds, reciting the blessing for "taking the *Lulav.*" He then turned the frantic sexton upside down and pronounced the benediction "and He has preserved us."

Concluding the ceremony, the miser put the sexton back on his feet and said to him:

"Now you should understand why I didn't want to give any money for the *Esrog* and *Lulav.* I don't like to fulfill the commandments of the Torah in an easy way."

IF WISHES WOULD COME TRUE

Wife: I wish that I were a *Mezuzah.*

Husband: Why?

Wife: Then you would also kiss me.

Husband: I wish that you were a *Lulav.*

Wife: What good would I do you then?

Husband: I would shake you on Sukkos and forget about you for the rest of the year.

As one does not fulfill his duty on Sukkos unless all four species are bound together, so Israel will not be redeemed unless all Jews hold together.

Yalkut 188a

Why is Sukkos called the Season of Our Rejoicing? Because Jews dwell in the *Sukkah* without their wives.

Folk Proverbs

On Sukkos one eats well but sleeps poorly. (One can eat everything but one must sleep in a *Sukkah*.)

He can be sent for a *Sukkah* gate. (A fool can be convinced to ask someone to loan him a *Sukkah* gate.)

The *Esrog* is more expensive but the blessing is said over the *Lulav*.

If one does not have an *Esrog*, he does not need a box.

He appears like a beaten *Hoshanna*. (One who goes about bowed down and dejected.)

On Hoshanna Rabbah at precisely midnight the heavens open and, if one utters a wish at that very moment, his wish will be fulfilled.

The Eighth Day of Solemn Assembly

The distinctive feature of Shemini Atzeres, the Eighth Day of Solemn Assembly, is the prayer for rain to enable the earth to produce its bountiful yield during the coming year. Since the rainy season starts about this time of the year in Israel, the farmer hopefully anticipates an abundance of it. While the recital of this prayer by Jews outside of Israel binds the destiny of their brethren in the Holy Land with themselves, its realization has not always proven helpful, as the following stories reveal.

A Prayer for Rain Is Answered

A severe drought wrought havoc with the crops. Unless rain would fall soon, the farmers would suffer great losses. The rabbi of the rural community decided to utilize the approaching festival of Shemini Atzeres, when it is customary to recite the "Prayer for Rain," to demonstrate the efficacy of prayer. To this end, he engaged a cantor to officiate for the festival.

On Shemini Atzeres morning the rabbi preached a soul-stirring sermon on the subject of prayer. Emphasizing that God always answers prayers that come from the inner recesses of the heart, he particularly urged the congregants to worship fervently to assure a favorable response to the "Prayer for Rain." With deep emotion the cantor chanted the special prayer and the congregation responded in like vein. Never before was such a "Prayer for Rain" heard.

No one was therefore surprised that a heavy rain descended as the services were concluded. It seemed as if the heavens were emptying, so abundant was the downpour. Surely, the rabbi was justified. Their prayers were answered generously.

In a short time, however, whatever had been left of the crops was completely destroyed by the over-abundance of water.

Two neighbors who had left their houses in the rain to examine their ruined fields met on the road. With a deep sigh of anguish, one said to the other:

"The rabbi really knows how to get answers to his prayers."

The other rejoined:

"That is quite true but he certainly doesn't know how to irrigate a field."

A Cantor's Successful Prayer

At the Shemini Atzeres services, the cantor rendered the "Prayer for Rain." He exploited every phrase and word of the prayer to display his vocal talents. No sooner was the prayer concluded than there was a downpour of rain.

After the service, the cantor braggingly remarked to the rabbi:

"I am pleased that God hearkened to my prayer and that I succeeded in causing rain to fall."

The rabbi quickly retorted:

"I am not at all surprised. Some time ago people like you caused a flood."

The Festival of the Rejoicing in the Law

Simhas Torah, the Festival of the Rejoicing in the Law, bears a twofold meaning: the Jew shall rejoice with the Torah and the Torah shall rejoice with the Jew. This festival rightfully becomes a day of feasting and merry-making for the Jew with whom the Torah rejoices. Some even hold that on this day it is permissible to drink more than usual. Indeed, it is the most joyous day of this most joyous season.

Simhas Torah marks the completion and

commencement of the yearly cycle of Torah
reading in the synagogue. Special ceremonies
attend the reading of the last and the first por-
tions of the Pentateuch. The persons honored
by being invited to recite the blessings over
these sections are called Hasan Torah (Bride-
groom of the Torah) and Hasan Bereshis
(Bridegroom of the Beginning). Hakafos (cir-
cuits) around the synagogue take place, the
men carrying the Scrolls of the Law to the
accompaniment of gay singing and dancing.
The children join the merry processions, bear-
ing high and waving Simhas Torah flags,
topped with lighted candles. Refreshments for
young and old climax the joyous celebration:
Thus, the supreme joy which reigns on Simhas
Torah has naturally saturated the wit and
humor associated with this day.

THE BRIDEGROOM OF THE TORAH

On Simhas Torah a rich though ignorant Jew was
given the honor of being called "Bridegroom of the
Torah." As the last portion of the Torah was being
read he stood alongside the reader under a canopy to
symbolize his marriage with the Torah-bride.

A learned Jew indignantly complained to the rabbi
that he permitted this ignorant man who was totally
unfamiliar with the Torah to be its groom, an honor
generally reserved for scholars.

The rabbi explained:

"Just as this ceremony is an ancient Jewish tradition,
so it was an old custom among Jews that the bridegroom

didn't know the bride until they met under the wedding canopy."

Rejoicing with the Torah

A Jew who was never able to find time to study was
seen rejoicing hilariously in the synagogue on Simhas
Torah. He sang and danced enthusiastically, ate and
drank abundantly, fully observing the Festival of the
Rejoicing in the Law.

Unable to fathom this sudden expression of love
for the Torah, the rabbi sarcastically said to the Jew:

"My friend, I'm engaged all year in the study of
the Torah and I have reason to be gay on this festival.
Why are you so joyous? Have you studied Torah all
year that you should now celebrate so ardently?"

The exhilarated Jew replied bluntly:

"On the Day of Atonement I smite my breast and
ask forgiveness for the sin of bribery. Am I guilty of
this sin? Am I an influential person? Am I a rabbi?
Why then should I confess a sin for which I am blame-
less? The reason is clear. It is written: 'All Israelites
are responsible for each other.' If I am responsible for
the sins of the rabbis, why shouldn't I take part in their
rejoicings?"

Observance of the Law Is Profitable

On the Festival of the Rejoicing in the Law a
notorious swindler was dancing in the synagogue with
a Torah clasped lovingly in his arms. The sexton, who
had had dealings with this character, asked him:

"Why are you so happy with the Torah? Did you

ever study it? Do you know what is in the Torah? Do you observe its commandments?"

"Why shouldn't I rejoice with the Torah?" the swindler rejoined. "The Torah has been most profitable for me. Let me tell you what happened. Some time ago I borrowed a hundred dollars from a neighbor. Asked to repay the loan, I denied that I ever received it. My neighbor hailed me before the rabbi. The sage thoughtfully considered the matter and declared that I must take an oath on the Torah. Of course, I didn't hesitate. I swore by the Torah that I never received the hundred dollars. Thereupon, the rabbi agreed that I didn't have to pay anything. Shouldn't I rejoice with the Torah?"

NO TIME FOR DANCING

In the general hilarity and confusion prevailing in the synagogue on Simhas Torah, the town's poor man danced with the town's rich man. The following day, confident that he had established a friendly relationship with the man of wealth, the pauper went to his palatial residence to secure a loan.

As the poor man entered the home of his newly-found friend, the latter immediately said to him:

"Did you come to dance with me? I'm sorry but I'm very busy today."

PREPARING THE WINE FOR SIMHAS TORAH

On the night following Simhas Torah, an emergency meeting of the members of the Tailors' Synagogue was convened to cope with a particularly depressing

situation. It was found on the Festival of the Rejoicing
in the Law that there had been insufficient wine to
celebrate properly. Many proposals were presented
to avoid the recurrence of such a tragic predicament.
Not one suggestion met with the approval of the tailors
and the debate continued until far into the night.
Finally, one of the more brilliant of the tailors offered
an astoundingly logical proposal. He suggested:

"Let an empty barrel be placed near the synagogue.
Every Friday each tailor will take a cup of his Sabbath
wine and pour it into the barrel. Thus, by next Simhas
Torah, we will have more than enough wine to observe
the festival fittingly."

This simple, equitable plan appealed to the tailors
and they readily accepted it. Each tailor promised faithfully to bring his cup of wine regularly on the eve of
every Sabbath.

With the arrival of the first Friday that the plan was
to go into effect, each tailor thought to himself:

"I'll pour a glass of water in the barrel and no one
will know the difference as it'll be diluted by the
abundance of wine."

The year passed. It was once again Simhas Torah.
The tailors were in their synagogue. They prepared
to drink *Le-hayyim*. The barrel was opened. Drinks
were poured for all. They recited the blessing for wine.
They sipped their cups. Lo and behold, they had pronounced a blessing in vain!

A Simhas Torah Celebration

Hasidim of the Baal Shem Tov were at his home
celebrating Simhas Torah with song and dance and

wine. Fearing lest they exhaust the supply of wine, the wife of the host complained to her husband:

"Tell your *Hasidim* to cease dancing and drinking for soon there will be no wine left for *Kiddush* and *Havdalah*."

With a smile on his lips, the Baal Shem Tov replied:

"You are undoubtedly correct. Tell them to stop and to go home."

The dutiful wife opened the door of the room where the *Hasidim* were rejoicing. When she witnessed the spiritual ecstasy that pervaded the atmosphere, she went and brought them more wine.

Later the Baal Shem Tov asked his spouse if she had told them to go home. She rejoined:

"You should have told them yourself!"

VIOLATING THE FESTIVAL

On Simhas Torah when Jews feel free to indulge themselves, a *Hasid* left the synagogue thoroughly inebriated. He stepped into the middle of the road and was unable to walk any further. To balance himself on his shaky legs, he spread them apart. A bull, charging down the road, caught the legs of the *Hasid* with his horns, flinging the unfortunate Jew over his back. As the bull continued on his way without diminishing his speed, the drunkard shouted:

"Jews! To the rescue! I am riding on a festival!"

A FESTIVAL FEUD IN HELM

The Jews of Helm were making plans to erect a new synagogue building. The "wise men" had already

resolved many weighty problems concerning the archi-
tecture of the building.

As they were about to commence the actual con-
struction, Berel, one of the most sagacious of the Helmites, suggested that the flooring of the synagogue be
planed smoothly. In support of his proposal, he called
attention to the fact that on Yom Kippur the wor-
shippers did not wear shoes and if the boards were not
smooth they would undoubtedly get splinters in their
feet.

Shmerel, another of the town's wise men, insisted
that if the flooring was smooth, the Jews would slide and
fall down when they danced in the synagogue on
Simhas Torah. He therefore argued that the flooring
should not be planed but that it should be left unfinished.

The sages of Helm fully recognized the seriousness
of the problem. It was not a matter to be taken lightly!
Everyone had an opinion to express on this contro-
versy. It did not take long for the city of Helm to be
divided into two warring camps. One camp supported
Berel and the other followed the leadership of Shmerel.

The Berelites importuned:

"Do you know what will happen to you if you get
a splinter in your foot? Your foot will become infected;
you will have to limp; and then you will fall anyway.
We must have a smooth floor!"

The Shmerelites protested thus:

"Do you know what will happen to you if you slide
and fall down on Simhas Torah? You will be dancing
with the Torah; you will have to drop the Torah; and
then you will have to fast for forty days. We must have
a rough floor!"

The building of the synagogue was held in abeyance
while the two factions waged a bitter battle. Days and
weeks and months went by but the war continued un-
abated. There appeared no hope of reaching an armi-
stice. The weary and battle-scarred warriors of Helm
finally appealed to the rabbi to negotiate a truce. The
rabbi listened to keen and forceful presentations by
both Berel and Shmerel. He then retired to his cham-
bers where he deliberated in solitude for seven days
and seven nights. On the morning of the eighth day,
he emerged from seclusion and summoned the leaders
of both armies. In an awe-inspiring voice he delivered
the decision that he had reached:

"For seven days and seven nights I considered your
claims. I consulted the books of law, the responsa of the
rabbis and the chronicles of Helm. I invoked divine
guidance. As a result I have come to the conclusion
that you are both right. I therefore decree that both
plans must be used. This is how it shall be done: the
floor boards shall be smooth on one side and rough on
the other. To avoid splinters on Yom Kippur, the
smooth side of the board shall be used. To prevent fall-
ing on Simhas Torah, the flooring shall be reversed
so that the rough side is on the surface."

And peace reigned once more in Helm.

HANUKKAH—FEAST OF LIGHTS

Kindling the Lights

CHAPTER FIVE

HANUKKAH—THE FEAST OF LIGHTS

*H*ANUKKAH, the Feast of Lights, recalls the dedication of the Temple in Jerusalem, following
the victory of the Maccabees over the Syrians. It brings
to mind a great moral victory rather than a military
triumph over defeated enemies. Thus, we read in the
Apocrypha:
"Judah and his brothers and the entire congregation
of Israel decreed that the days of the dedication of the
altar should be kept with gladness and joy at their due
season, year after year, for eight days from the twenty-
fifth of the month of Kislev" (I Maccabees 4.59).
When the perpetual lamp of the Temple was to be
lit at the dedication, only one small cruse of undefiled
oil, for the needs of a single day, was found. But it
lasted for eight days! To mark this miracle, the Hanukkah menorah is kindled on each of the eight days of
the festival. An old folk proverb sums it up (to be said
with a shrug of the shoulders): "For such a little bit of
oil such a big festival is celebrated!"
While the candles slowly burn, hymns are sung. Games
with the Dreidel, a spinning top, are played, for it is
forbidden to do work by the light of Hanukkah's can-

*dles. The holiday is further enlivened by the distribu-
tion of Hanukkah Gelt (money) and the exchange of
gifts. As each festival has its special dish, so Hanukkah
has its distinctive delicacy—Latkes (potato pancakes).
A proverb explains the reason for the eating of this
delicacy—"Hanukkah's Latkes teach us that one cannot live by miracles alone."*

KINDLING THE LIGHTS

On the first night of Hanukkah, a five-year-old native
of Tel Aviv carefully observed his father light the
candle on the Hanukkah lamp and intone the benediction:

"Blessed art Thou, O Lord our God, King of the
Universe, Who hast sanctified us by Thy commandments, and commanded us to kindle *the light* of Hanukkah."

The following evening the boy requested that he be
allowed to light the two candles for the second night
of the festival. He assured his father that he knew the
proper blessing. His proud father willingly complied
with the son's request. Holding aloft the *Shamash*
candle as high as his small hand could reach, he chanted:

"Blessed are Thou . . . Who . . . commanded us
to kindle the *two lights* of Hanukkah."

A CANTOR COLLECTS HANUKKAH GELT

A superannuated cantor had been pensioned by his
congregation for he was still well-liked, even though he
had lost his once sweet voice. To add to his meagre

pension he took advantage of every possible opportunity to secure the emoluments that were formerly due him as cantor.

Hanukkah was traditionally a particularly propitious season for him. He would visit the homes of the members of the congregation to wish them a joyous holiday. Naturally, they would return his greetings and present him with the customary Hanukkah *Gelt*.

One year the cantor found that his age was creeping up on him and he was unable to get about as speedily as in previous years. Moreover, at every home that he visited he was urged to rest for a while, to eat *Latkes* and to join in the Hanukkah rejoicing. He soon realized that he was making slow progress and he feared that if he dallied too long in each one he would be unable to visit all the homes to collect his Hanukkah *Gelt*. He finally hit upon an idea.

At the next house he approached, the cantor stood on the threshold and called:

"A happy Hanukkah to all of you! I'm very busy tonight as I have many people to visit. If you'll not give me my Hanukkah *Gelt* immediately and allow me to depart, I'll begin to sing."

LATKES WITHOUT INGREDIENTS

In the town of Helm on the first night of Hanukkah, when families were gathered for the gay festivities, a childless widow was alone in her home. Although she was quite well-to-do, she was extremely miserly.

Her solitude on this particular night was disturbed by a sudden knock on the door.

"Who is there?" she asked.

"It is I," a voice replied. "I am a student of the *Yeshivah*. I come from Pinsk. My name is Hayyim."

As the widow hesitatingly opened the door a trifle, Hayyim unhesitatingly pushed it open further and entered the house without waiting for a formal invitation.

The startled widow retreated and exclaimed:

"Go away! Leave me alone! What are you doing here?"

Hayyim spoke in a calm and soothing tone:

"Don't be afraid of me. I have come to spend the evening with you. All the students of the *Yeshivah* are celebrating Hanukkah with their families. Only I have no family. Knowing that you, too, were alone, I decided to keep you company. Together we can enjoy the festival."

Regaining her composure, the widow said:

"It's very kind and thoughtful of you. How shall we celebrate Hanukkah?"

"If you'll make *Latkes*, I'll sing to you some Hanukkah ditties," Hayyim proposed.

Although her larder was well-stocked, the niggardly widow protested:

"I have nothing with which to make *Latkes*."

The hungry Yeshivah student had already observed the luxurious furniture in the room and the costly jewelry the widow was wearing and he was not to be sidetracked from his determination to eat *Latkes*. In a voice full of profound sympathy, he said:

"It is indeed a pity that you don't have even the few ingredients needed to make *Latkes*. That doesn't matter. I'll show you how to make this delicacy with nothing."

This proposal of Hayyim appealed to the widow's miserliness.

"Of course," Hayyim glibly continued, "I really can't make *Latkes* with *absolutely* nothing. Do you have a piece of scrap iron?"

Intrigued, the widow produced the scrap iron.

Hayyim washed the iron thoroughly and set it in a large bowl. Then he poured water into the bowl and stirred for five minutes. Then he tasted the water.

"Um! So far so good!" he testified. "If you would have had a few eggs, then the *Latkes* would really be delicious."

The widow's curiosity overcame her stinginess. She decided that it might be worth while to use some eggs if she could learn how *Latkes* are made from scrap iron. She went to the pantry, took out the eggs and handed them to Hayyim.

Hayyim poured the water out of the mixing bowl, replaced it with the eggs and beat them for some time. Then he tasted the mixture.

"Um! So far so good!" he testified again. "If we had some flour, then the *Latkes* would *really* be delicious."

The widow's curiosity had gone too far to turn back now. So she went again to the pantry and took out a bag of flour and handed it to Hayyim.

Hayyim poured the flour into the bowl and stirred for some time. Then he tasted the concoction.

"Um! So far so good!" Hayyim repeated once more. "If we had a bit of salt and a little oil, then the *Latkes* would *really and truly* be delicious."

Once more the widow's curiosity prevailed over her instinct and she decided that it might even be worth while to use a bit of salt and a little oil if she could finally learn how *Latkes* are made from scrap iron. So she went once again to the pantry and took salt and oil and handed them to Hayyim.

Hayyim poured salt into the bowl and stirred for a while. Then he tasted the new mixture.

"Um! So far so good!" Hayyim repeated again. "Now all we need is a fire."

He lit the stove, rubbed the oil on a pan, poured in the mixture and, presto! in a few minutes there were sizzling hot *Latkes*.

Hayyim and the widow sat down at the table and ate the delicious *Latkes*. When they finished, he began to sing Hanukkah songs and the widow took the dishes into the kitchen. In a flash she returned, exclaiming:

"The iron! The iron did not melt! It is still in the bowl."

Hayyim did not answer. He finished the ditty he was singing and, as he was about to leave, said:

"Take good care of the iron. When I return tomorrow night, we'll make more *Latkes* from it. A happy Hanukkah to you!"

A WOEFUL PLIGHT

Berel: I'm in a frightful predicament. I don't know how I can fulfill the duty of eating *Latkes* on Hanukkah. If I eat less than five *Latkes,* they will not satisfy me. If I eat five or more *Latkes,* I'll be a glutton. What would you advise me to do? Please help me out of this terrible plight.

Shmerel: There is indeed a simple solution. Make one *Latke* as big as five *Latkes.*

"Never Postpone for Tomorrow"

On the day before Hanukkah, a solicitous mother said to her son:

"You should do your homework now. Tomorrow is Hanukkah and you'll want to play with the *Dreidel*. Never postpone for tomorrow that which you can do today."

"If that's so," the child coyly responded, "give me the Hanukkah *Latkes* that you prepared for tomorrow."

Mother's Latkes

Leah: I'll bet you that my mother's *Latkes* are better than those your mother makes.

Rachel: My mother's *Latkes* are so delicious that even though I ate them several hours ago I still have the delicious taste in my mouth.

Leah: Not only do I have the taste of my mother's *Latkes* in my mouth even though I ate them yesterday but I can still feel them in my stomach.

A Hanukkah Lesson in School

In a school in Tel Aviv a teacher was presenting the historical background of the festival of Hanukkah to her pupils. She described the glorious struggle of the Maccabean brothers and stated that the outstanding hero among them was Judah Ha-Maccabee. At this point one pupil excitedly exclaimed:

"No! No! Not Judah Ha-Maccabee but Judah Ha-Poel." *

* The Maccabee and the Ha-Poel are the major sports organizations in Israel.

Ignoring the interruption, the teacher told about the conflict between the Israelites and the Syrians.

It was then that another pupil curiously inquired:

"On which side did the Americans fight?"

The teacher patiently explained that the war occurred two thousand years ago. She then resumed the story and called particular attention to the role played by the Syrian ruler, Antiochus:

"Antiochus, who was called both Epiphanes (illustrious) and Epimanes (madman), persecuted the Jews and introduced Greek culture in Palestine. If he were alive today, why would he be considered an unusual tyrant?"

A bright lad promptly raised his hand. When the teacher recognized him, he replied forthrightly:

"If Antiochus were alive today, he would certainly be considered unusual. He would be more than two thousand years old!"

Fortunately the bell rang and the teacher dismissed the class, wishing the pupils a happy Hanukkah.

A SLIGHT MIXUP

During the festival of Hanukkah, a young lady of Tel Aviv visited a cooperative colony in the Emek. Her face, generously covered with rouge, lipstick, mascara and powder, was an unusual sight in this workers' settlement.

A bright native child of six, staring in bewilderment at the strange face masked by the cosmetic make-up, turned to his mother and asked:

"Why is it that today, when we observe Hanukkah, in Tel Aviv they celebrate Purim?"

Hanukkah Gifts

A teacher was telling his pupils that during Hanukkah they should receive a gift on each night of the holiday as part of the candle-lighting ceremony and celebration. Just as the brightness increases with each additional candle, so should the joy with each gift.

True to form, one pupil wanted to know:

"Why isn't it exactly as with the candles? One gift the first night, two gifts the second night and so on . . ."

The Spelling of Hanukkah

"What use does the letter G serve in the word Hanukkah?"

"In Hanukkah there is no G."

"Why shouldn't there be a G in Hanukkah?"

"What use would the letter G serve in Hanukkah?"

"That's the question I am asking you!"

What is it that has one foot and cannot stand but it can dance?

A Hanukkah *Dreidel*.

PURIM—FEAST OF LOTS

Purim Masqueraders

CHAPTER SIX

PURIM—THE FEAST OF LOTS

*T*HE story of Purim (the Feast of Lots) as found in
*the Scroll of Esther tells how the Jews in ancient
Persia, with the guidance of Mordecai and Esther, the
Jewish queen of Ahasuerus, emerged triumphant from
an impending doom at the hands of Haman. This Scroll
apparently made a strong appeal to the rabbis of the Talmud and Midrash for they added rich embellishments
to it.*

*"With the arrival of Adar one should be exceedingly
joyful" (Taanit 29a), our sages have ordained, for that
is the month in which Purim occurs. The observance of
the Purim festival brings joy and hope and faith to the
Jew. It is a day for regaling the body with good things
and for drinking, as it is written in the Talmud: "A
person is obligated to drink on Purim until he knows
not the difference between 'Cursed be Haman' and
'Blessed be Mordecai'" (Megillah 7b).*

*Purim's very joyousness marks the Jew's reaction to
near destruction. His wit and humor in connection with
this holiday eloquently voice the escape from high ten-
sioned experiences that separate life from death.*

Mordecai the Linguist

In the days of Nicholas I, when the Russian government sought to introduce the Jews to secular culture, Rabbi Moses Landau, a Jewish scholar and well-versed in many other fields of learning, was one of the first Jews to accept the government's plan. Moreover, he became a strong advocate of spreading "Enlightenment" and used every opportunity to preach this program to Jewish communities.

One day the rabbi assembled the people of his city in the synagogue and spoke to them about the religious duty to learn the language of the land. He cited proofs from the Bible and the Talmud to show that their ancestors approved the study of foreign tongues. He quoted profusely from the Book of Esther. Among other things, he said:

"It is well known that the miracle of Purim was made possible because Mordecai heard the plotting of Bigthan and Teresh, who sought to kill King Ahasuerus, and reported it to Queen Esther. If Mordecai had not been able to understand the language of these two chamberlains, the series of events that led to Purim would not have occurred and the Jews would have been annihilated . . ."

"You are mistaken," interrupted one of the Jews of the congregation. "What you say proves that the Jews did not know the language of Persia. The two chamberlains, Bigthan and Teresh, spoke unhesitatingly in the presence of Mordecai which shows they had no reason to suspect that he understood them."

Haman's Bribe

During the time that Joseph Dov Ber Soloveitchik
served as rabbi in Brisk, the government issued a disastrous order which compelled the Jewish storekeepers
to close their shops. A meeting of all those affected was
convened to seek a way to overcome this harsh decree.
After a thorough exploration of all possible means to
have the edict annulled, it was finally decided to offer
a substantial bribe to the responsible government offi-
cials. The storekeepers agreed to collect among themselves enough funds for the bribe. A committee was
chosen to take up the collection.

As each storekeeper was approached by the committee
for his share of the bribe, he refused to give anything,
claiming that the other merchants could afford it more
than he.

Frustrated, the committee revealed the situation to
Rabbi Joseph Dov Ber. The rabbi immediately summoned the storekeepers to his home. When they were
all assembled, the sage reminded them of the story of
Purim which brought an immediate and generous response from the merchants. This is what he said to them:

"Now I understand why Haman succeeded in having
Ahasuerus, who was not an evil king, issue a decree to
kill all the Jews. Haman offered the king ten thousand
talents of silver for the privilege. If the wealthy Jews had
offered the king twenty thousand talents of silver, he
certainly would have annulled his edict without further
ado. The Jews of Persia were wise enough to understand this situation and agreed to make such an offer.
However, when the committee came to collect money,

each Jew said: 'I am unable to contribute. Let the others give.' "

A One-Day Plot

A: Why did Haman try to destroy all the Jews in one day? He could have extended the time by devising various tortures.

B: Haman feared lest the Jews might somehow triumph and he did not want them to celebrate for more than one day.

The Beauty of Esther

On the Saturday afternoon before Purim, the rabbi of the cobblers' synagogue was discoursing on the Scroll of Esther. Among the many legends he related was one which told that Esther was not beautiful.

A cobbler interrupted the rabbi to ask:

"If Esther was not a beauty, why did Ahasuerus select her for his bride?"

Another cobbler sitting alongside the inquisitive one pulled the latter's sleeve and whispered in his ear:

"You fool! Do you really think that Ahasuerus waited until our rabbi gave him his opinion on the beauty of Esther?"

Fasting on a Festival

Esther ordered Mordecai to proclaim a fast of three days beginning on the eve of Passover. Mordecai was perturbed at such a request and asked:

"How can we desecrate the festival of Passover by fasting on it?"

Esther replied:
"If there be no Israel in the world, who will observe
the festivals?"

Midrash Panim Aherim

LOTS

The teacher explained to the class that *Pur* means
"lot" and *Purim* is "lots." As a homework assignment
the pupils were instructed to look up the meaning of
"lots."

The next day the teacher asked the class what they
had learned about Purim. Avi raised his hand and was
called upon to recite. In a well-rehearsed tone he said:

"LOT, the nephew of Abraham, had LOTS of LOTS,
and LOT had a LOT of trouble with his wife, and what
a LOT was hers! We expect to have LOTS of fun on
Purim."

NO MOURNERS FOR HAMAN

The *Kaddish,* the mourner's prayer, is recited following the reading of the scrolls of the *Song of Songs, Ruth*
and *Ecclesiastes.* Why is it not said after the recital of
the scroll of *Esther?*

All of Haman's sons were hanged and there was no one
to say *Kaddish* for him.

Sending of Portions and Gifts to the Poor

*Purim is a time of "sending portions one to
another and gifts to the poor" (Esther 9.22).
Maimonides wrote in his Mishneh Torah: "It*

is better to increase the gifts to the poor than
to make for oneself a big meal or to send more
portions to friends, for there is no greater or
nobler joy than to gladden the hearts of the
poor." In the fulfillment of these duties, the
Shalah Monos Treggers, the messengers who
bear the portions and gifts, play an indispen-
sable role which has earned for them a unique
place in Jewish folklore. The poor, too, have
an important share. As it is commanded to give
charity on Purim, they do a favor to their
well-to-do brethren by accepting it. Hence, the
proverb, "On Purim no one says: 'Thank you'."

A Weak Memory

A rich man forgot to send a Purim gift to his son's
Melamed (teacher). Although the latter sent him a gen-
tle reminder through the pupil, he still neglected the
customary present for the teacher.

Shortly after Purim, the *Melamed* told the pupil to
ask his father this question:

"Why did Abel kill Cain?"

The pupil obediently did as he was instructed and on
the following day the father came running angrily to
the teacher and shouted:

"Ignoramus! How can you ask such a question? It was
Cain who killed Abel."

"Is that right?" the *Melamed* retorted quietly. "Such
an ancient episode you can remember, but to send a
Purim gift to your son's teacher, although I reminded
you only a few days ago, that you could not remember."

Exchanging Purim Gifts

When the Malbim was rabbi in Bucharest he had many antagonists among the elders of the city who sought to make his life miserable by every possible means.

Once, on Purim, one of his enemies, a rich and insolent man, sent him a Purim gift on a tray covered with a white napkin, according to the usage of the day. When the Malbim removed the napkin, he found on the plate a baked confectionary in the shape of a pig. He smiled and thought to himself: "How affectionate are my townsmen for they spare food from their own mouths and send it to their rabbi!"

To fulfill the commandment of "sending portions" and to reciprocate in kind, the Malbim took a picture of himself and placed it on a plate, covering it with the napkin. He gave it to the messenger to return to his congregant with a note which read:

"You were kind enough to send me a likeness of yourself, so, as a fair exchange, I am sending you one of myself."

Another antagonist sent the Malbim, as a *Shalah Monos*, a portion of ham, properly covered with a white napkin. The Malbim promptly acknowledged receipt of this gift by sending a letter of appreciation in which he wrote:

"Your Purim gift is indeed an expression of your warm friendship for me as you undoubtedly took the food that you eat yourself and sent it to me."

An Unwelcome Gift

It happened to be the week before Purim when the rabbi paid a visit to the town's dentist. The dentist found it necessary to extract a tooth from the rabbi's mouth. Although the rabbi offered to pay the dentist, he refused to accept any fee, saying:

"Let this be my Purim gift to you."

The rabbi laughingly replied:

"I appreciate your generosity but please keep this matter as a secret between us. I am afraid that if other Jews will hear about it, they will want to honor me on Purim by pulling out the rest of my teeth."

Riches on Purim

A bridegroom was being interviewed by his rich prospective father-in-law who asked, among many other questions, what he earned. The young man answered:

"I earn ten rubles a day."

Satisfied that his daughter would have the comforts to which she was accustomed, the bride's father consented to the marriage.

In due course the wedding ceremonies took place. After the wedding, the father-in-law was astonished to learn that his new son-in-law was not employed and, in great anxiety, he asked him:

"Why aren't you working? You informed me that you earn as much as ten rubles a day!"

"I didn't deceive you," the son-in-law reassured him. "I'm an experienced *Shalah Monos* messenger and I receive large gratuities for my services. On the one day of the year when I work, I earn at least ten rubles."

ORANGES FOR PURIM

The Jews of Helm were most zealous in the observance of Purim, particularly with regard to *Mishloah
Monos*. Every Helmite would send gifts of sweets and
baked goods and fruits to his relatives and friends. For
the rabbi and the *rebbetzin* each Purim plate bore a
golden apple—that rare delicacy, usually reserved only
for the wealthy. Of course, the rabbi and his *rebbetzin*
could never afford to buy oranges and, if it were not for
Purim, they would never taste this delectable fruit.

One Purim a severe catastrophe struck the Jewish
community of Helm. Grief and consternation prevailed
in the town.

May Jews never know any more of such sorrow! Do
you want to know the calamity that befell the sainted
rabbi and his wife? Do you want to know what brought
this heavy affliction upon the Helmites? I will not keep
you in suspense any longer. But do not be unduly
alarmed, for just as the Jews of Persia in the days of
Mordecai and Esther were saved from impending doom
by their ingenuity so were the Jews of Helm spared.

As I was saying, it happened on Purim. The *Shalah
Monos Treggers* of Helm felt neglected that they were
not recipients of oranges. So they decided to take the
law into their own hands and to right this grievous
wrong. What did they do? They used a simple expedi-
ent. They merely confiscated the oranges from the Purim
plates intended for the beloved rabbi and *rebbetzin*.
Imagine the consternation of the spiritual leader and
his spouse when they received *Mishloah Monos* without the golden apples!

The following year with the approach of Purim, the

elders of Helm convened an assembly and deliberated at great length. Many diverse and unique plans were proposed and discussed to avert a recurrence of the tragic event of the previous year. Finally, it was unanimously resolved to engage armless men as *Shalah Monos Treggers* so that they would be unable to take the oranges. Thus it was done. On Purim the plates were tied with strings around the necks of the messengers and they were despatched to their destination. The armless messengers were not so easily diverted. On the way they met friends and asked them to remove the oranges from the plates and to hide them in their pockets.

The ruse of the wise Helmites was foiled! Once again the rabbi and the *rebbetzin* were orangeless. Their sorrow, shared by the elders of the community, was profound and persisted throughout the entire year.

The following year with the approach of Purim, the elders of Helm convened an assembly and deliberated at great length. Many diverse and unique plans were proposed and discussed to avert a recurrence of the tragic event of the previous year. Finally, it was unanimously resolved to engage men who were not only armless but also dumb so that they would not only be unable to take the oranges but they would also be unable to ask anyone to remove them from the plates. Thus it was done. On Purim the plates were tied with strings around the necks of the messengers and they were despatched to their destination. The armless and dumb messengers were not so easily diverted either. On the way they met friends and by winking with their eyes indicated that they wanted them to remove the oranges from the plates and to hide them in their pockets.

Again the ruse of the wise Helmites was foiled! Once

again the rabbi and the *rebbetzin* were orangeless. Their sorrow, shared by the elders of the community, was profound and persisted throughout the entire year.

The following year with the approach of Purim, the elders of Helm convened an assembly and deliberated at great length. Many diverse and unique plans were proposed and discussed to avert a recurrence of the tragic event of the previous year. Finally, it was unanimously resolved to engage men who were not only armless and dumb but also blind so that they would not be able to wink to their friends. Thus it was done. On Purim the plates were tied with strings around the necks of the messengers and they were despatched to their destination. The armless, dumb and blind messengers were not so easily diverted. They walked straight to their own homes and their wives removed the oranges from the plates.

Again the ruse of the wise Helmites was foiled! Once again the rabbi and the *rebbetzin* were orangeless. Their sorrow, shared by the elders of the community, was profound and persisted throughout the entire year.

The following year with the approach of Purim, the elders of Helm convened an assembly and deliberated at great length. Many diverse and unique plans were proposed and discussed to avert a recurrence of the tragic event of the previous year. Finally, it was unanimously resolved to engage men who were not only armless, dumb and blind but also legless so that they would not be able to walk to their homes. Thus it was done.

But, you may ask, how did the *Shalah Monos Treggers* walk to the home of the rabbi? This was a simple matter. Those who engaged the messengers to take the Purim gifts to the rabbi carried them on their shoulders.

This ingenious solution proved most satisfactory. Henceforth, on every Purim the rabbi and the *rebbetzin* enjoyed golden apples and the city of Helm "shouted and was glad. The Jews had light and gladness, and joy and honor."

GIFTS FOR THE POOR

One Purim, Rabbi Abraham Joshua Heshel of Apta was seated in his study and receiving guests who brought him, among other items, money as Purim gifts. After each guest departed, the rabbi carefully counted and fondled the coins he had received. Noticing this unusual interest in money, his son asked him:

"Father, I know only too well how you despise money and that you really do not understand its value. Why are you gloating over these coins you have received?"

"Let me explain to you my sudden interest in this money," the rabbi replied. "With this money I will fulfill the commandment of giving gifts to the poor on Purim. If I show no regard for the money, then my gifts will be meaningless."

AN OPEN BOOK OR AN OPEN HAND

One Purim, Rabbi Joseph Saul Nathanson of Lemberg saw a rich scholar sitting in the *Bes Ha-Midrash* and studying the Talmud. The rabbi approached him and unceremoniously took away the volume in which the rich man was engrossed.

"Today your place is not in the House of Study before an open book," chided Rabbi Joseph Saul. "You should be at home before a plate full of money to dis-

pense charity with an open hand to the poor who come
to you."

CHARITY ON SHUSHAN PURIM

On Shushan Purim, Rabbi Shalom Rokeah of Belz
gathered together the poor people of his town and distributed charity to each one of them. He used to say:

"On Shushan Purim the Jews neglect the needs of the
indigent. As it is a *Mitzvah* to give 'gifts to the poor' on
Purim, which Jews do generously, they erroneously assume that they have fulfilled their duty and are not required to continue to dispense charity."

ON SHUSHAN PURIM

On Shushan Purim, the day following the Feast of the
Lots, a simple, pious Jew went to his rabbi and wrath-
fully complained:

"I'm coming now from the market place where I saw
many Jews making purchases. If they had fulfilled the
commandment of giving gifts to the poor yesterday, how
is it that they have money today?"

The rabbi calmed him in a soothing tone, explaining:

"You are mistaken in your deduction. The Jews who
are buying today were the poor of yesterday."

The Purim Seudah

Purim is a day of "feasting and gladness"
(Esther 9.22). The obligation to eat, drink and
be merry on the Feast of Esther compelled the
creation of new delicacies for both Mishloah

Monos (the sending of gifts) and the special Purim Seudah (meal). Kalonymus ben Kalonymus, the fourteenth century Italian Jewish parodist, lists in his Tractate Purim twenty-four meat and pastry dishes that "were told to Moses on Mount Sinai, all of which one must prepare on Purim." The festive Purim meal features not only wine, but also triangular-shaped Kreplach (dough filled with meat) and the pièce de résistance—Hamantashen (cakes filled with poppy seeds).

True Repentance

A Jew was seen by his neighbor eating a hearty meal in a public place on the Fast of Esther. The latter took him to task, saying:

"Even weak and elderly people do not eat on the Fast of Esther unless they have to do so, and then only in private. I am amazed that you, a young and healthy person, eat publicly on this fast day."

"I'm not observing this fast," the accused replied. "I don't believe that Mordecai was justified in refusing to bow down before Haman, thus jeopardizing the lives of the Jews of Shushan."

On the following day, the neighbor noticed that the Jew was enjoying the Purim *Seudah,* eating *Hamantashen* and drinking wine as was customary on Purim. Again he protested vehemently:

"If you favored the appeasement of Haman and violated the Fast of Esther, how is it that you partake of the Purim *Seudah* which commemorates the downfall of Haman?"

"Indeed, my actions may seem strange to you," the Jew replied. "Yesterday I was in full accord with Haman; but, upon listening to the reading of the *Megillah* last night, I realized that Mordecai had acted properly. So I repented my error and I decided to observe the Purim feast today."

A BOTTOMLESS PIT

A *Hasid* was privileged to have as a guest of honor for his Purim *Seudah* a distinguished grandson of a sainted *Rebbe*. When the wife of the *Hasid* placed the traditional *Kreplach* on the table the grandson took one and said:

"I'm taking one to recall our God who is One alone in heaven and on earth."

He then took two and said:

"I'm taking two to recall Moses and Aaron."

He then took three and said:

"I'm taking three to recall the three patriarchs—Abraham, Isaac and Jacob."

He then took four and said:

"I'm taking four to recall the four mothers in Israel —Sarah, Rebecca, Rachel and Leah."

He continued until he finally reached twelve *Kreplach* and said:

"I'm taking twelve to recall the twelve tribes of Israel."

The host, seeing that the guest's appetite was not yet satisfied and that he was prepared to continue devouring the *Kreplach*, hastened to summon his wife.

"Leah, come quickly and remove the plate of *Kreplach*, as I suspect that our guest may desire to recall the six hundred thousand Israelites who went forth from Egypt."

Hamantashen Are Hamantashen

Judy: Why are *Hamantashen* called *Hamantashen?*

Sarah: Because they are made with *Man*—poppy seed —and the *Man* is placed in *Tashen*—pockets.

Rebecca: Because they are made in the shape of the three-cornered hat worn by Haman.

Judy: You are both wrong. They are called *Hamantashen* because they look like *Hamantashen* and they taste like *Hamantashen!*

Purim Wine

On the night of Purim Hershele Ostropoler arrived home in a state of intoxication. He was piously observing the festival for he had reached the condition of one "who does not know the difference between 'Blessed be Mordecai' and 'Cursed be Haman.'"

Fearful that his wife would not permit him to enter his house, he knocked on the door with both hands and shouted:

"Hurry! Open the door! I bought a barrel of wine!"

Hershele's wife, who was not adverse to observing the festival with drink, hastened to open the door. Seeing her spouse standing on the threshold empty-handed, she asked:

"Where's the barrel of wine that you said you bought?"

Hershele, patting his stomach, explained:

"I didn't have a barrel so I poured the wine into my stomach."

THIRTY-THREE

The sixteenth century rabbi, Moses Isserles of Krakow, lived thirty-three years, wrote thirty-three books and died on the thirty-third day of the Omer. At his funeral the speaker delivering the eulogy sought to enumerate thirty-three virtues of the deceased. He recited thirty-two and was at a loss for another virtue to complete his eulogy.

The sexton of Rabbi Isserles came to his assistance by citing this practice:

"On the night after Purim during the festival meal, Rabbi Moses would go from house to house to remind the inhabitants to pray the evening service which they were likely to forget due to their preoccupation with the enjoyment of eating and drinking. He would enter a house, request water for washing his hands, and say, as if to himself, 'It is time to pray the evening service.' Having reminded the people, he would go on to the next house."

Masquerading

Masquerading on Purim is an old custom which, though frowned upon by some rabbis, others felt was a fitting manner to enhance the joyousness of the day. The practice of masquerading gave rise to the "Purim Rabbi" in the Yeshivos who would wittily mimic the heads of the academies.

THE PURIM RABBI

At the famous *Yeshivah* of Wolozin Purim was celebrated with much gaiety and frolicking. Among the most popular customs was the appointment of one of the students as Purim Rabbi. He was dressed in clothes worn by the head of the *Yeshivah* and would imitate the latter's habits and ways of instruction. Once, while the Purim Rabbi was delivering a learned discourse, he inadvertently besmirched the honor of the head of the *Yeshivah*, Rabbi Naphtali Tzvi Yehudah Berlin.

On the following day, Shushan Purim, the ex-Purim Rabbi, realizing that he had insulted Rabbi Berlin, went to confess the sin and to seek pardon.

"Please don't be angry with me as I didn't know what I was doing yesterday," he replied.

"I have nothing against you," the rabbi replied. "However, I want to tell you something. There is a saying: 'What is on a sober man's lung [heart] is on a drunkard's tongue.' If this is true, why is it necessary to go to so much trouble to examine the lung of an animal after its slaughter to determine if it is *Kosher?* It would be much simpler and more convenient to examine the lung before slaughtering by giving the animal wine to drink. Then an inspection of the tongue should reveal if there is any adhesion on the animal's lung. From this instance we learn that the saying refers only to a man and not to an animal."

MASQUERADING

Why is the Day of Atonement called in Hebrew *Yom Ki-Purim,* a day like Purim?

The similarity between the two days is based on the fact that on both days it is customary to masquerade. On Purim, Jews masquerade and don the costumes of non-Jews. On the Day of Atonement, they masquerade as pious Jews.

A PURIM MIRACLE

A Purim rabbi related the following miracle:

"On the Day of Atonement, we were seated at the *Seder* table chanting the Book of Lamentations. Suddenly, the Hanukkah lights were extinguished by the wind as the door of the *Sukkah* was opened and the Purim players entered blowing *Shofars*. The following night, being Shavuos, the heavens opened up and Sabbath *Hallos* descended upon the *Bimah* where the *Hasan Bereshis* was reciting the afternoon service."

THE PURIM TO COME

While Hitler was delivering one of his infamous speeches in a large hall in Munich at the start of the Nazi ascent to power, he could not help but notice that a man in the front row was making facial contortions of derision and joy, marked with an occasional outburst of laughter.

The man's behavior resulted in bringing confusion to Hitler in the midst of his antisemitic invectives and causing annoyance to the *Fuehrer*. After the speech, Hitler sent for the man and indignantly asked who he was.

"I am a Jew," he said innocently.

"Then you should be taking my address more seriously," warned Hitler. "Don't you believe that I will fulfill my threats to bring about the destruction of the Jews?"

"You should know," the Jew replied, "that you are not the first antisemite who sought to destroy us. You may recall that the great Pharaoh of Egypt sought to enslave the Jews. To commemorate his defeat and our redemption, we eat tasty *Matzos* and observe the festival of Passover. Haman was another enemy of ours who brought about his own downfall. The delicious *Hamantashen* we eat and the jolly festival of Purim recall our deliverance from him. While listening to your venomous diatribe, I wondered what kind of delicacy the Jews would invent and what kind of holiday they would establish to celebrate your downfall."

FOLK PROVERBS

On Purim everything is permissible.

Today is Purim, tomorrow it's o'er;
So give me a penny and show me the door.

Twilight on Purim means pitch darkness on Passover. (Whoever cannot afford to pay for the simple needs of Purim will be in much worse circumstances for Passover with its costly requirements.)

Purim drives dull care away.

After a Purim meal no dog goes hungry. (The remnants of the Purim meal suffice plentifully for the dogs.)

All year drunk and on Purim sober!

It will last as long as from the Fast of Esther to Purim.

Less out of "the love of Mordecai" than of "the hatred of Haman."

On Hanukkah and Purim the poor become rich. (It is on these holidays that they receive gifts.)

Not on every Purim does a miracle happen.

When Purim comes, one forgets all troubles.

Hamantashen that appear in a dream are really not *Hamantashen*.

Everything is permissible on Purim, though after the holiday the fool becomes known.

He had Haman's fall!

He grows like a Purim *Keylitsh*.

He wrote a long *Megillah*.

He listens to his neighbor as Haman listens to the *Groger*.

People listen to the *Megillah* just as they listen to the rabbi; they listen to the rabbi just as they listen to the *Megillah;* and they listen to both just as they listen to last year's snow.

PASSOVER—FESTIVAL OF FREEDOM

Searching for Leaven

CHAPTER SEVEN

PASSOVER—THE FESTIVAL OF FREEDOM

*P*ASSOVER *commemorates the exodus of the children of Israel from Egyptian bondage. It is another joyous festival. Following the miraculous crossing of the Red Sea, Moses and the Israelites sang a song of praise to the Lord and Miriam and the righteous women danced with timbrels. Thus the redemption was celebrated by the former slaves.*

During the reign of Hezekiah, King of Judah, "the children of Israel that were present at Jerusalem kept the feast of unleavened bread seven days with great gladness; and the Levites and the priests praised the Lord day by day, singing with loud instruments unto the Lord" (II Chronicles 30.21).

During the "Season of Our Freedom," as Passover is called, we observe the sacred nature of freedom with great prayers and beautiful ceremonies. But we also eat, drink and rejoice in remembrance of the liberation from slavery.

Of all the festival days, excluding the Sabbath, Passover has elicited unending stories of delightful fun and trenchant wit and humor. This is understandable precisely because of what is at stake in Passover—love of liberty and devotion to freedom, the dignity of the hu-

*man being and the hatred of tyranny. What more subtle
way to fight the evils of slavery and dictatorship than to
hold them and their works up to ridicule and mockery
and blow away their pretentions in gales of laughter?*

FOR THE SAKE OF RIGHTEOUS WOMEN

A *Magid* in the course of preaching on *Shabbos Ha-
Gadol,* the Sabbath preceding Passover, said:

"The Talmud states: 'For the sake of the righteous
women that were in that generation the children of Israel were redeemed from Egypt.' What did the Talmud
mean?

"It is known that the Israelites should have remained
in slavery in Egypt four hundred years, as it is written
in the book of *Genesis:* 'And they shall afflict them four
hundred years.' However, they were enslaved there only
two hundred and ten years. The question is: Why was
their period of bondage shortened?

"The answer is to be found with the righteous women.
They complained to the Almighty that they missed their
men folk and beseeched Him to redeem them. God reminded them that the time for redemption had not yet
arrived as they were scheduled to be enslaved for nearly
two hundred years more.

"Then the righteous women said: 'We are prepared
to assume responsibility for our husbands. If You will
place them in our hands, we promise You that they will
continue to be slaves.'

"The Almighty readily granted their request. That is
the reason the Talmud says: 'For the sake of the righteous women . . . the children of Israel were redeemed
from Egypt.' "

Girls After the Boys

The Bible reveals that Pharaoh commanded that every Hebrew male child should be cast into the river. If Pharaoh intended to annihilate the children of Israel, why did he not order the girls as well as the boys to be drowned?

Pharaoh knew that if all the boys would be thrown into the river, the girls would jump in after them.

The Route of Moses

Joe, a college freshman, desired to flaunt his newly acquired wisdom in the face of his pious father. With an air of profundity, he remarked:

"My professor told us that Moses did not have any knowledge of geography. If he had, he would have led the children of Israel from Egypt to Palestine in a week instead of forty years."

The father, who lacked the benefits of higher education, shook his head slightly and replied:

"Perhaps Moses did not know geography but I am certain that your professor does not know the Jews. If he had been in the place of Moses, he would not have brought the Jews to the Land of Israel even in forty years. The professor would never have taken them out of Egypt!"

The Crossing of the Red Sea

One day a lover of art brought home a large canvas in an ornate frame. Displaying it to his wife with deep pride, he said:

"Look at this beautiful Passover painting I bought!"

The wife stared in amazement at the canvas for it was completely blank.

"I do not see anything on this canvas. Did you buy it at the Gallery of Modern Art?" the wife naïvely inquired. "What is it supposed to be?"

"This is a painting of the Jews crossing the Red Sea," the spouse replied condescendingly.

"But where are the Jews?"

"The Jews already passed through the sea and they are on the shore."

"And where are the Egyptians?"

"The Egyptians are still pursuing the children of Israel and they have not yet reached the sea."

"And where then is the sea itself?"

"The waters of the sea are divided and have receded to the shores so that the Jews should be able to cross."

AFTER THE CROSSING

Teacher: What did the children of Israel do after they crossed the Red Sea?

Pupil: They removed their clothes and hung them up to dry.

DIVIDING THE WATERS

A Jew had invited a beggar to his home to partake of a Sabbath meal. The beggar was not at all shy and, as soon as the *Kiddush* was recited, he began to pour for himself drink after drink of his host's best whiskey. He emptied each glassful of schnaps by dunking pieces of the delicious, white *Hallah* and devouring them.

The host was truly bewildered. He feared greatly that the beggar would finish both the *Hallah* and the whiskey and not leave any for his family. Desiring to restrain the beggar without offending him, he said:

"I don't understand why it was necessary for Moses to divide the mighty waters of the Red Sea. If he had given pieces of *Hallah* to the children of Israel, they would have been able to dry the sea by dunking the *Hallah*."

"That would have been possible," the beggar retorted, momentarily interrupting his drinking and dunking. "Unfortunately, the Rea Sea was divided on Passover when the Jews are not permitted to handle and certainly not to eat *Hallah*."

A RELIGIOUS DISPUTATION

Rabbi Jonathan of Prague engaged frequently in religious disputations with a local priest. One day the priest said to him:

"Let us for once change our positions in a debate. I will defend the Jews and you can speak in behalf of the Christians."

Rabbi Jonathan reluctantly agreed to this strange proposal. The priest then said:

"Both Jews and Christians observe their own Passover festivals. We, the Jews, celebrate Passover for our ancestors were enslaved by Pharaoh in Egypt and were redeemed by the Lord. But, why do you, Christians, observe this festival?"

The brilliant rabbi hesitated only for a minute and then replied:

"The festival of Passover is celebrated by us Chris-

tians because, if the children of Israel had not been delivered from Egyptian bondage, there might not have
been any Jews in the world and we would not have had
our messiah."

Preparation for the Festival

*When spring is in the air, the Holiday of
Spring, another designation for Passover, is not
far off. Preparations for the festival begin
weeks in advance for there is much to do. Baking of Matzos was an exciting event in Old
World Jewish communities. "Spring cleaning"
keeps the housewife busy. New clothes need to
be bought. New dishes and all the special foods
must be purchased. All in all, the numerous
and elaborate preparations create an atmosphere of gay anticipation and occasionally of
grave concern for those who lack the wherewithal to celebrate the Passover properly.*

PREPARING PASSOVER PROVISIONS

"I'm in great distress," an indigent Jew complained to
his rabbi. "With the approach of Passover, I find that
I don't have any provisions so that I might observe the
festival as it is incumbent on a pious Jew."

"Don't worry," the sage said reassuringly. "The Mu-
nificent One will surely provide for His children."

"Rabbi, I do have faith in God yet I am beset with
so many worries that I fear they are more than I can
bear. I need *Matzos,* wine, chicken, other foods and
clothing for my wife and children."

"Perhaps I can help you," the rabbi suggested. "Let's figure how much you really need. How much will *Matzos* cost?"

"Two rubles."

"And wine?"

"Four rubles."

"And chicken?"

"Five rubles."

"And the other foods?"

"Four rubles."

"And clothing for your family?"

"Twelve rubles."

"Let me see. Altogether you need for Passover twenty-seven rubles. You can now stop worrying about everything except how you will get the twenty-seven rubles. It's really not so bad. All you have is one worry."

No Need to Worry

Immediately after Purim a poor man came to the spiritual head of his congregation and implored him:

"Rabbi, help me! In a month from now Passover will be here and I don't have any money to buy wine and *Matzos*."

"There's still plenty of time until Passover," the rabbi spoke reassuringly. "You shouldn't worry. You will have wine and *Matzos* for Passover."

The Jew felt relieved by the rabbi's words of reassurance and returned home with his mind completely at ease.

Two weeks later, on *Rosh Hodesh* Nisan, he went again to the rabbi, complaining:

"Rabbi, help me! In two weeks from today Passover

will be here and I still don't have any money to buy wine and *Matzos*."

Once again the sage did not hesitate to reassure him:

"I've already told you that you will have provisions for Passover. Don't worry."

The poor man, sadly disappointed this time, returned home in a mood of despair and frustration. Another week passed by and there was still no sign of Passover provisions. Now his wife began to complain bitterly. Reluctant as he was to face the rabbi again, he felt compelled to do so.

He meekly approached the rabbi once again and repeated his dilemma. The rabbi became exceedingly angry and chided him:

"Do you doubt my word? Don't you have any faith? Go home and relax. You will have wine and *Matzos* for Passover."

The eve of Passover finally arrived and there were still no wine and *Matzos*. The man took the silverware that he used during the entire year to the marketplace and sold it. With the proceeds he bought wine, *Matzos* and all the other provisions needed to observe the festival properly.

That night, when he arrived in the synagogue, the rabbi asked him:

"Well, do you have wine and *Matzos?*"

When the poor man told the rabbi what he was compelled to do, the sage responded:

"Well, I told you that you would have provisions for Passover, didn't I?"

THE RABBI'S PASSOVER NEEDS

With the arrival of Nisan, a rabbi complained to his wife that he was overwhelmed with problems.

"What are you worried about?" the *rebbetzin* solicitously inquired.

"I have two big worries," the rabbi explained. "First, I need a sermon for the Great Sabbath preceding Passover. Second, I need money so that you can purchase food for the festival."

The *rebbetzin* quickly retorted:

"Don't worry about the sermon. You can use the same one you delivered last year. No one will remember what you preached. On the other hand, you should worry about the money for the Passover food since the storekeepers will surely remember that I still owe them last year's bill."

HALF-READY

Knowing that Hershele Ostropoler was very poor, hardly ever having enough food for a meal in his home, Hayyim asked him if he had made the necessary provisions for Passover. Hershele replied that he had prepared half of the provisions and the other half God would provide.

Amazed to learn of Hershele's sudden good fortune, Hayyim inquired how he had succeeded in securing these provisions.

"Don't be so surprised," Hershele answered. "You know that there are two major requirements for Passover. First, no leaven shall be seen in a Jew's house and, second, one must eat unleavened bread. The first I have already fulfilled as leaven has not been seen in my house for a long time. As I have done fifty percent of the requirements, I now rely on the All-Munificent One who will surely provide me with *Matzos* and other foods for Passover."

The Removal of Hametz

During the week preceding Passover, a lad observed with fascination the elaborate preparations his mother was making for the festival. The progressive parent was anxious that her offspring understand why she was thus busily engaged.

"Do you know why I am so diligent in the removal of all bread from the house and why we will have only *Matzos* next week?" the mother asked.

The bright boy immediately replied:

"Oh, sure! It's because you are going on a diet."

Supervising the Matzah Baking

Rabbi Israel Lipkin Salanter was most meticulous in the baking of *Matzos* for Passover. To make certain that everything was done according to the strictest interpretation of Jewish law, he personally undertook to supervise the baking.

One year Rabbi Salanter was bed-ridden and unable to go to the bakery. He instructed two pupils to go in his stead.

As the pupils were about to depart for their assigned task, they asked their teacher:

"Is there anything special which we should watch?"

"Yes," the rabbi replied. "See that the old woman who does the mixing is paid sufficiently. She is a poor widow."

EARNING THE PASSOVER SUPPLIES

A few days before Passover, Motke Habad of Vilna went to the tailor's shop, seated himself comfortably in a corner and fell asleep.

A customer entered the shop and was surprised to see his friend Motke. Shaking Motke, he awoke him and asked:

"What are you doing here, Motke?"

In a voice loud enough for the tailor to hear, Motke said:

"I'm helping the tailor who is very busy this week. With the approach of Passover he is loaded with work and he doesn't have time to rest. Since I have enough time, I came here to rest for him. I hope that for my helping him the tailor will give me wine and *Matzos* for Passover."

HOW TO ENJOY THE FESTIVAL

Rabbi Naphtali Tzvi Yehudah Berlin of Wolozin was usually lenient in his interpretation of Jewish law and he expressed concern for those who strove to enforce the laws strictly. One Passover he explained the reason for his leniency.

"On Passover I am truly able to fulfill the commandment: 'Thou shalt rejoice in thy festival.' I am content that I have fulfilled all of the obligations for its observance. Those who seek a more stringent application of the festival traditions are undoubtedly in a constant state of anxiety and worry. They fear lest the search for leaven was inadequate, that the *Matzos* were not baked properly, that the wine is not strictly *Kosher*. Therefore, it is impossible for them to have peace of mind and to enjoy Passover."

Maos Hittim

The funds for the Passover needs of the poor are called Maos Hittim, money for wheat for Matzos. Weeks before Passover, collections are taken up by the rabbis and communal leaders to provide the extraordinary festival necessities for the indigent. Appeals are made in the synagogue and sometimes house to house collections are undertaken. Many Jewish communities have organized special societies for this purpose. This obligation has been readily assumed for the Jew cannot conscientiously celebrate the joyous festival when he knows that his brethren are unable to celebrate. Reluctance on the part of wealthy Jews to provide Maos Hittim is the subject of some caustic anecdotes.

MONEY FOR THE POOR

A charity warden went to the home of a rich Jew on the eve of Passover to solicit *Maos Hittim*. He rapped on the door, awaking the affluent one from his afternoon siesta. Angry that his nap was disturbed, the rich Jew opened the door in a sour mood. His mood was translated into action when he saw the warden and he slapped his face. The warden placed one hand on his face to soothe the stinging pain and extended his other hand to the rich man, saying:

"The slap you gave to me. Now, what will you give to the poor?"

AN UNINTENTIONAL PROMISE

The need for funds to supply Passover foods for the poor of the community was so great that the rabbi himself undertook to go from house to house to take up a collection. When he arrived at the home of the town's most affluent Jew—a notorious miser—he found him ailing.

The miser, fearing for his life, beseeched the rabbi:

"Please pray for me that I may recover from my illness before Passover. If I get well, on the eve of Passover I'll give you a hundred rubles to distribute to the poor."

The rabbi hastened to the synagogue and assembled a *Minyan* of Jews. They recited Psalms and prayers for the sick. With God's help, the skinflint recovered. Early in the morning on the eve of Passover, the rabbi returned to the palatial home of the rich Jew and said to him:

"Our prayers in your behalf have been granted. Thank God that you are once again enjoying good health. Now, you can give me the one hundred rubles for the poor you promised if you would recover from your illness."

"Did I make such a promise?" the miser asked in a tone of innocence. "If I did, that only proves how critically ill I was."

CHARITY BEGINS AT HOME

A delegation of the *Maos Hittim* Society visited a
wealthy Jew to solicit a contribution. In eloquent and
moving words, they described the dire need of the poor
who would be unable to observe Passover if they would
not be given aid. Unmoved by the stirring appeal, the
rich man said:

"I regret that I am unable to do anything for them.
I want you to know that my own brother is very poor."

The following day when the society was distributing
Matzos to the poor, some of the members were astonished to see the brother of the wealthy Jew standing
in line. They refused to give him anything on the
ground that his wealthy brother claimed that he supported him. The poor man protested vehemently that
his brother never gave him anything.

Thereupon, the leading members of the society
went to the rich man again and angrily asked him to
explain his deceit.

"Did I claim that I was helping my poor brother?"
the miser asked. "I only said that my own brother is
very poor. Now that you know that I don't support
him, how can you expect me to give assistance to those
who aren't my kin?"

A POOR ORPHAN

The representative of the *Maos Hittim* fund was
disappointed with the niggardly donation of the town's
wealthiest Jew. He reproached the man in a caustic
tone:

"This is too small a contribution for such an important *Mitzvah*. Even your son, who is really poor in comparison with you, gave a much larger amount of money."

The rich man was not stirred and retorted cleverly:

"How can you compare me with my son? He has a rich father while I am an unfortunate orphan."

No Need to Search for Hametz

Rabbi Eizel Harif of Slonim, while soliciting *Maos Hittim,* came upon an affluent but stingy Jew removing the leaven from his clothing. Although the sage vividly described the plight of the poor people for whom he was collecting funds, his plea fell upon deaf ears. The wealthy Jew continued to search for *Hametz.* As he began to examine his pockets, the rabbi said to him:

"You don't need to search for *Hametz* in your pockets. Your refusal to heed my request is proof that you're a Jew only as far as your pocket."

Milk at the Seder

A local Jew came to Rabbi Akiva Eger of Posen on the eve of Passover.

"Rabbi, I've a ritual question to ask you," he said. "Is it permissible to use four cups of milk at the *Seder* instead of four cups of wine?"

"Why would you want to substitute milk for wine? Are you, God forbid, ill?"

"No, rabbi. I am well but I can't afford to buy wine."

The discerning rabbi then said:

"I'm sorry. It is forbidden to use a substitute for wine." Reaching a hand into his pocket, he continued: "Take these twenty rubles and purchase wine."

After the Jew had left, the *rebbetzin* angrily chided her husband:

"Why did you give him twenty rubles for wine? Two or three rubles would have been sufficient."

"Don't be angry," the rabbi asked. "The fact that this poor man was prepared to drink milk at the *Seder* is evidence that he also didn't have money to buy meat and perhaps not even fish and *Matzos*. With the twenty rubles he will be able to observe the *Seder* properly."

BARON ROTHSCHILD AS MESSENGER

The eve of Passover had arrived and Shmuel and his pious wife Rivkah were bemoaning their dire poverty and especially their lack of earthly goods required for the proper observance of the festival. They considered many ways to cope with their tragic plight but none seemed suitable. Finally, Rivkah prevailed upon her husband to appeal directly to the Almighty and to despatch a letter to Him explaining their predicament. Shmuel wrote an appropriate missile and cast it to the winds with a prayer on his lips that the message may soar aloft to His Heavenly Abode.

Baron Rothschild happened to be riding in his carriage in the neighborhood and noticed the letter laying on the road. When he read the urgent appeal, his deepest sympathy was aroused. He sent his servant with a hundred rubles to give to Shmuel.

The servant delivered the money in the name of

Baron Rothschild. Without a word of appreciation to the servant or the Baron, Shmuel turned to his wife and said:

"See, Rivkah. God has sent Baron Rothschild as His messenger. I wonder how much Rothschild deducted for his expenses."

A FIFTY PERCENT SUCCESS

When Naphtali Tzvi Horowitz, the Ropshitzer *rebbe*, returned home from the synagogue on the Sabbath before Passover after delivering a *Shabbos Ha-Gadol* discourse, his wife noticed that he appeared very tired and depressed. When she asked him why he looked so haggard, Rabbi Naphtali said:

"I exerted myself strenuously in the delivery of my discourse. Anxious to arouse the sympathy of our rich brethren so that they would provide the poor with the requisite Passover provisions, I spoke with much emotion and at great length."

"Were your efforts successful?" the rabbi's wife inquired solicitously.

"I'm certain that I had at least a fifty percent success," the rabbi sighed. "I'm not certain that the rich Jews will give to the poor but I'm quite certain that the poor are ready to accept if they will only be offered something."

A DISCOURSE ON MAIMONIDES

On the Great Sabbath preceding Passover, Rabbi Mendele of Linsk said in the course of his sermon:

"On *Shabbos Ha-Gadol* it is customary for rabbis in

their sermons to try to resolve difficult questions and seeming contradictions that are found in the works of Maimonides. I will not depart from this tradition.

"Maimonides affirms that the law requires every Jew, even the poorest, to eat *Matzos* on Passover. He also agrees that it is forbidden to steal. Now, I ask you: 'What shall the poor Jews who do not have money to buy *Matzos* do if they are not permitted to steal?' The answer to this apparent contradiction is really simple: 'The rich Jews must give money to the poor so that the poor will not violate the commandment on stealing and so that they will be able to fulfill the injunction to eat *Matzos* on Passover.'"

A SIYUM FOR THE FIRST-BORN

After the morning services on the eve of Passover, the congregants waited impatiently for the rabbi to commence the *Siyum*, the ceremony of a discourse on Torah and a festive meal which accompanies the conclusion of the study of a sacred book. By participating in this prescribed meal the congregants would be released from observing the fast incumbent upon first-born sons to recall that God slew the first-born of the Egyptians but spared those of Israel. The rabbi sat at the head of a long table, flanked on both sides by the congregants, attentively attuned to the words of Torah they expected to hear. The sage, however, was deeply engrossed in the volume that lay before him and did not utter a word. The Jews, anxious to return home so that they could burn the *Hametz* in due time and conclude the Passover preparations, were impatient.

Finally, the rabbi, with a deep sigh, said:

"I am advancing in age and I no longer have the strength to deliver a discourse as has been my practice on this occasion. I will therefore be very brief. This is my message: 'There are many poor Jews in our midst who do not have any money for their Passover needs. I will not make a *Siyum* until you will give me one hundred rubles for the poor.' "

The short and sharp presentation proved effective.

Eating of Matzah

The eating of Matzah on Passover is a reminder of the hasty departure of the children of Israel from Egypt which did not allow them to prepare food for the journey and they were only able to bake unleavened cakes. Matzah is also called "bread of affliction" to recall the hardships of Egyptian slavery. The Matzos, made by hand before machines were used, were often thick, hard and not easy on the teeth, as may be learned from some of the following stories.

UNEXPECTED GENEROSITY

One year a wealthy, miserly Jew amazed the local townsmen by distributing *Matzos* in large quantities to the poor. Although the unleavened bread was thick and hard, the recipients of this windfall did not mind, especially as they received as much as they wanted.

Only after the festival of Passover did the people understand the reason for the man's munificence. His son, who had returned home from the university where he had earned a diploma and license, hung a shingle on the front of the house which read:

Maximilian Levy, Dentist

EATING MATZOS

Rabbi Zundel of Salant was critically ill. When the doctor came he found the patient unconscious. He made his diagnosis and concluded that the only cure was to remove all the rabbi's teeth, which he proceeded to do. The rabbi's condition then improved rapidly. Regaining consciousness, he noticed that his teeth were missing. With a deep sigh, he lamented:

"Alas, how will I be able to eat *Matzos* on Passover?"

A PREFERENCE FOR MATZAH

The lord of the manor was in financial straits and borrowed money from a Jew for which he gave a note. When the day came for the note to be redeemed, the creditor appeared at the manor to claim his money. Inasmuch as the situation of the lord had not changed, he informed him that he was unable to fulfill his obligation. When the man indicated that he would appeal to the local authorities, the lord whipped out a revolver, pointed it in the face of the quaking Jew, and said threateningly:

"Either you'll swallow the note or I'll kill you!"

Without the necessity for any further remonstrances, the Jew obediently put the note in his mouth and swallowed it.

Subsequently the baron obtained funds and paid his debt.

Some time later, during the festival of Passover, the lord of the manor summoned the Jew again to negotiate another loan. The latter brought with him a piece of *Matzah* and requested the lord to write the note on it.

The confounded lord shouted:

"Are you crazy? What's the meaning of this?"

"I'm afraid that when I return at this time next year for you to redeem the loan I may have to eat the note. As it will again be Passover, I won't want to eat anything that may be leaven. Furthermore, *Matzah* is more digestible and tastier than paper."

MATZAH IS MATZAH

Why is *Matzah* called *Matzah?*

Because it has the shape of *Matzah;* it has small holes like *Matzah;* it is dry as *Matzah;* it tastes like *Matzah.* What else can you call it but *Matzah?*

The Disposal of Hametz

All leavened bread and food, as well as all dishes and cooking utensils used throughout the year, must be removed from the home for Passover. The use of certain items, such as peas and beans, while generally forbidden, was occasionally permitted. On the night before Passover, the "Searching for Hametz," which the head of the family performs by candle light, is a picturesque and fascinating experience for the children. They are usually given the privilege of "Burning the Hametz"

*on the following morning. The Hametz that
is not burnt must be sold to a non-Jew by
means of a legal bill of sale so that none
remains in Jewish possession during the festival. However, it may be bought back from
the non-Jew after Passover.*

DISPOSING OF THE HAMETZ

Joshua was quarreling with his wife Deborah on the
eve of Passover. Taunting her, he said:

"I sold all the *Hametz* except you."

"You need not be concerned about me," Deborah
retorted promptly. "Many years ago my father sold
me to a non-Jew."

LAW-ABIDING JEWS

On the eve of Passover, Rabbi Levi Isaac of Berditchev summoned a group of business men who he
suspected were engaged in smuggling goods across the
border. In a harsh tone, he asked them:

"Do you have any smuggled goods?"

"Plenty, rabbi," they readily admitted.

He then inquired:

"Do you have any *Hametz* in your homes?"

"God forbid, rabbi," they protested. "We already
sold all of our *Hametz*."

Levi Isaac then lifted his gaze on high and said:

"Father in Heaven! See how wonderful the Jews
are! The mighty Czar of Russia, who has an army, a
police force and prisons, has forbidden the people to
smuggle; yet, they pay no attention to his law and

publicly violate it. But You have forbidden the children of Israel to have *Hametz* on Passover and, even
though You do not have an army or police force or
prisons, they obey Your commandment!"

FOOD FOR SOLDIERS

Rabbi Samuel Mohilever was interested in the wel-
fare of Jews who served in the army and his congregation had accepted the responsibility for supplying those
who were stationed in the town with *Kosher* food.

One year a drought had caused a severe food shortage.
The *Parnas* of his congregation asked him what could
be done to have the necessary *Kosher* provisions for
the approaching Passover.

Rabbi Mohilever replied:

"Although it is not usual, I will permit the eating of
peas on Passover."

Greatly relieved, the *Parnas* said:

"Now we'll be able to feed the soldiers peas."

The rabbi, resenting the easy solution of which the
Parnas was ready to take advantage, quickly replied:

"That I will not permit in our community. You and
I, as well as all the congregants, will be permitted to eat
peas; however, for the Jewish soldiers we must provide
only the most strictly *Kosher* and the best food for the
festival."

BEANS PERMITTED

In a year of famine, Rabbi Isaac Elhanan Spektor of
Kovno was told that many poor people would be unable to have food for Passover because of the high cost

of everything except beans. Although it was well-known that the use of beans on Passover was questionable, the rabbi unhesitatingly stated that he permitted eating them. When he was questioned about his leniency, he replied:

"I, too, will eat beans this Passover. Then the poor people won't have any feelings of guilt."

Determining Permissible Foods

A newly arrived rabbi in America was faced with the problem of determining the permissible foods for Passover. He discussed the subject with numerous people and, after a thorough investigation, he reached this conclusion:

In view of the fact that in America there is so much falsehood and deceit, the foods that are supposed to be *Kosher* for Passover are certainly forbidden, while such items as bread and beer must be permissible. The bread is not really bread and the beer is not really beer.

No Matzah for the Litvaks

The *Maos Hittim* committee was in a quandary. The funds available for *Matzos* for the poor were hardly sufficient to provide for half of those who applied. The members of the committee, all Polish Jews, decided that the *Matzos* would be distributed only to the Polish Jews and the Litvaks would be compelled to make their own arrangements.

When this plan was reported to the rabbi of the community, himself a Litvak, he said:

"I am in full agreement with this proposal."

The rabbi's sexton was outraged to hear this ready acquiescence.

"Rabbi," shouted the sexton, "do you want to have our brethren desecrate the festival by eating bread?"

"I have no such fears," the Litvak rabbi replied. "If the Polish Jews will not have any *Matzos*, I am sure that they will eat bread. I am equally certain that the Litvaks would prefer to starve on Passover rather than eat bread."

HERSHELE IS VANQUISHED

Hershele Ostropoler went to visit an old friend and was disappointed to learn from the wife that his friend had left town for a few days. This situation did not prevent Hershele from seating himself comfortably in an easy chair and patiently waiting for the spouse to invite him to dine. After waiting in vain for an hour, he said sympathetically:

"It's too bad that your husband left you alone on Purim."

"Alas," the woman sighed. Then she asked, "If today is Purim who will read the Scroll of Esther for me and who will conduct the Purim meal?"

Hershele gallantly offered to do both. When he had finished the reading of the *Megillah* and, of course, partaking of a delectable feast, he wished his hostess a merry Purim and departed in a joyous mood.

Upon the friend's return, his wife severely berated him for leaving her alone on Purim and lauded Hershele for making it possible for her to observe the festival according to Jewish tradition.

The man readily understood Hershele's intrigue but he decided to bide his time. One month later he met Hershele in the street and graciously invited him to his home for a drink. The wit naturally accepted the cordial invitation. After entering the house, the host gave Hershele some beer. When the latter had imbibed to his capacity, the friend arose and, without any warning, slapped Hershele on both cheeks, exclaiming:

"Sinner! How dare you indulge in drinking beer on Passover?"

"But today isn't Passover," Hershele, utterly confused, protested.

"If a month ago was Purim, today must be Passover," the friend said in triumphant vengeance.

A Passover Transaction

A Jewish tavern owner complained to Rabbi Meir of Premislan during the intermediary days of the Passover festival:

"In accordance with the laws of Passover, I sold my tavern to a non-Jew for the duration of the festival. I just went to observe how he was handling the business. Do you know what he is doing? The money he receives he puts into his pockets instead of into the cash register. I'm fearful that, by the time Passover is over, I'll sustain a heavy loss."

The rabbi advised the tavern owner:

"You should tell the non-Jew: 'The tavern and its income belongs to you. Therefore there's no need for you to steal the money you receive.'"

Before It Is Too Late

Hayyim Nahman Bialik, the late Hebrew poet laureate, came upon several agnostics eating bread on the afternoon of the last day of Passover and said to them:

"You had better hurry lest you prolong your meal and Passover may be over before you finish eating. Then you will no longer be committing a sin and it will be permissible for you to eat bread."

The Haggadah

The Haggadah, which literally means "narration," is a special book read at the Passover Seder. It includes the story of the holiday, appropriate passages from the Bible, prayers and folk songs. So endeared to the people has this small book become that over two thousand editions have been printed, many with quaint and beautiful illustrations. Hundreds of commentaries have been written and some exegetists have not hesitated to make emendations to the text. It is therefore not surprising that, among others, the Jews of Helm in their infinite wisdom also saw fit to emend the Haggadah.

A Commentary on the Haggadah

An author of a commentary on the Passover *Haggadah* requested a letter of endorsement from a rabbi. The latter carefully examined the manuscript but he was unimpressed with its merit.

"I think that there have already been published plenty of commentaries on the *Haggadah*," the rabbi gently said.

The author indignantly protested:

"You, above all people, should know that from all the other commentaries I can't earn the necessities for Passover."

THANKS ARE NOT ENOUGH

On the eve of Passover, an editor of a new edition of the *Haggadah* brought his work as a "gift" to a prosperous man. The latter casually perused it and then said:

"I'm glad to have this book. Please accept my thanks for it."

"You are indeed welcome to it," the author rejoined. "Now, I would like to ask you the question: Why is 'A Psalm of Thanks' not recited on the eve of Passover?"

The wealthy Jew said that he did not know the answer and the editor continued:

"On the eve of Passover when many sacrifices were due one could not fulfill his duty with mere thanks."

DAYENU

A self-appointed committee of Jewish laymen were deeply engrossed in preparing a new, abbreviated *Haggadah* which would be more suited to modern times. Having already made considerable deletions, they were discussing what to do with the song *"Dayenu"*

("It would have been sufficient"). One of the men proposed that it be completely omitted. There was immediate disagreement. Following a lengthy discussion, a compromise was finally reached. They agreed to retain the following passages:

"If He had given us their money and not given us the Torah, it would have been sufficient."

THE HAGGADAH OF HELM

Once upon a time the *Haggadah* of the Jews of Helm was the same as the *Haggadah* of the Jews throughout the world and had the following words: "The Torah spoke about four sons—one is wise, one is evil, one is simple and one does not know how to ask."

An inspiration came to the Helmites and they realized that it was truly unnecessary for the *Haggadah* to say "one is wise." It would be clearer to say "one is a Helmite" and all would understand that a wise man is intended. Thereupon they printed a new edition of the *Haggadah* with the textual emendation so that it now read: "The Torah spoke about four sons—one is a Helmite . . ."

After several years, a new inspiration came to the Helmites which made them realize that it was truly unnecessary for the *Haggadah* to say "one is a Helmite." It would be clearer to say "one is wise" and all would understand that a Helmite is intended. Thereupon they printed new *Haggadahs* with the textual emendation so that it now read: "The Torah spoke about four sons—one is wise . . ."

Since then the *Haggadah* of the Jews of Helm has been the same as the *Haggadah* of the Jews throughout the world. However, in a commentary written by a sage of Helm, there will be found this interpretation:

A wise son—a Helmite.

THE RABBIS OF THE HAGGADAH

On the eve of Passover, Hayyim was homeward bound with a new *Haggadah* that he had promised to buy for his wife. Passing a tavern, he dropped in to quench his thirst. He found, however, that one drink was insufficient for the purpose and ordered a second and a third. When he found that he didn't have enough money to pay for all the whiskey he had imbibed, he was forced to leave his new *Haggadah* as surety.

When Hayyim arrived home, his spouse asked him for the new *Haggadah* that he had gone to purchase.

"Listen, I'll tell you what happened," Hayyim began to explain. "I bought a beautiful *Haggadah* for you and I was tempted to examine it while walking home. I was delighted to find that the *Haggadah* had great rabbis—Eliezer, Joshua, Eleazer ben Azariah, Akiva and Tarphon. So I invited them to join me in a drink that we might all recite a blessing and wish each other '*Le-hayyim*' on the eve of Passover. So we entered a tavern and we drank and wished each other '*Le-hayyim*.' Unfortunately, the rabbis were weak and became drunk. So they remained in the tavern and I came home alone."

The Passover Seder

The Seder, the order of the ceremonies for the first two nights of Passover as found in the

*Haggadah, is a gala family occasion. The color-
ful rites, the gay songs and festive meal create
an atmosphere of joyous abandonment. And,
just as the Jew cannot have selfish enjoyment,
so he must not forget those less fortunate than
himself. Thus, the opening paragraph, following the Sanctification, states: "Let all who are
hungry, enter and eat; let all who are needy,
come and celebrate the Passover with us."
Then, too, he is not permitted to rejoice over
the downfall of enemies. That is the reason
why, when the ten plagues are enumerated,
the drops of wine are spilled out of the cup
to symbolize that our cup of salvation is not
full.*

CONDUCTING THE SEDER

Velvel Vinshinsky had recently moved to a town
with a Jewish community after having lived for more
than a score of years in a small, Russian village. Isolated
from other Jews, Velvel had become lax in the observance of Jewish laws and customs. Indeed, he had
forgotten most of them. Now, that he dwelt amongst
his brethren, he was anxious to fulfill all the obligations incumbent upon a Jew.

With the approach of Passover, Velvel observed that
his fellow-Jews were buying new clothes and so he
followed suit. In addition, he purchased all the special
Passover foods that he saw in the stores. However, on
the eve of Passover, he was sorely distressed. He hadn't
the faintest notion of how to conduct a *Seder*. And his
wife was of no help in this regard.

Velvel decided to have his wife look into their next-door neighbor's window so that she could see how a *Seder* is conducted. What she saw there caused her no end of anguish. The neighbor slapped his wife's face vigorously and shouted at the top of his lungs: *"This* is Passover! *This* is a *Seder! This* is a festival!" Believing that the scene she had witnessed was a *Seder,* the woman, considerably depressed, returned to her house. Fearing that Velvel would also slap her if she reported to him what she had witnessed, she remained silent. Although Velvel asked her again and again to report to him what she had seen, the frightened spouse was speechless.

After much useless prodding, Velvel lost his patience and, in great anger, he slapped his wife's face, shouting: *"This* is Passover! *This* is a *Seder! This* is a festival!"

While the chastised woman was smarting from the sting of her husband's unexpected blows, she was amazed at the erudition of Velvel.

"If you knew how a *Seder* is conducted, why did you send me to our neighbor to see what they do?" the wife meekly complained.

A Gracious Host

Rabbi Akiva Eger was zealous about offering hospitality and was especially scrupulous about fulfilling the injunction for the Passover *Seder:* "Let those who are hungry enter and eat with us."

Once at the *Seder* table a guest accidently tipped over his goblet of wine. To spare the visitor from any embarrassment, Rabbi Akiva surreptitiously and quickly moved the table, and knocked over his own cup of wine and remarked apologetically:

"It seems to me that the table is not standing properly."

THE TEN PLAGUES

An ignorant Jew and his wife were observing the *Seder*. When the time came to enumerate the ten plagues, the woman found it necessary to go into the kitchen. The Jew, proceeding with the service, decided that it was incumbent upon him to pour out a drop of wine for each plague not only for himself but also for his wife. So doing, he said:

"Blood for me, blood for my wife; frogs for me, frogs for my wife; lice for me, lice for my wife . . ."

The Fours

Four Sons—Four Questions—Four Cups. These fours have prominent places in the Haggadah. There are the four sons of different dispositions—the wise, the wicked, the simple and the one who does not know how to ask a question. However, there is always one, usually the youngest child, who does know how to ask and he raises four questions related to the distinctive character of Passover. Then there are the four cups filled with wine, symbols of joy, which recall the four promises of redemption that God made to the children of Israel. About these "Fours," so reminiscent of days of de-

*spair and hope, the tense mood produces its
inevitable relief in wit and humor, each in
accord with the experiences of its generation.*

FOUR CUPS OF WINE

Hayyim the *Hasid* and Mendel the *Misnagid* were
disputing the relative merits of their respective sects.

Mendel claimed that Moses the Lawgiver was a
Misnagid for he gave the Torah to the Jews so that they
could study.

Naturally, Hayyim could not accept this argument.
As evidence that Moses was a *Hasid*, he pointed out
that the lawgiver did not command the study of four
chapters of the Torah on Passover but he did provide
for the drinking of four cups of wine.

NEEDED IMPROVEMENTS

A connoisseur of wines once remarked:

"If I had been Moses, I would have improved upon
the Passover arrangements. I would have given the
Egyptians only four plagues and I would have provided
for the Jews ten cups of wine."

HAD GADYA

The rabbi, passing the town's slaughter house, observed the *Shohet*, who was in a state of intoxication,
killing an ox. The infuriated rabbi forthwith forbade
the slaughterer to engage in his profession. Friends of
the latter besieged the rabbi and pleaded with him
to forgive the slaughterer and permit him to resume

his work. The rabbi was obdurate and refused to budge from his decision. He explained to them:

"In the song 'Had Gadya' that is sung at the conclusion of the Seder, we learn that 'the Angel of Death killed the Shohet who had slaughtered the ox . . .' Why was the slaughterer slain since he had only performed his duty? The answer is that the Shohet killed the ox after he had drunk the four cups of wine at the Seder."

A Proper Seder Celebration

The Passover Seder was over and Rabbi Levi Isaac of Berditchev had retired for the night. His sleep was interrupted by a startling dream. An angel appeared to him and said:

"Levi Isaac of Berditchev, you should not rest easy! Do you think that you observed the Seder properly? Yankel is the one who is truly observing Passover!"

The following morning at the synagogue Levi Isaac inquired as to the identity of Yankel. When he learned that Yankel was a blacksmith, he approached him and asked:

"Please tell me how you celebrated the Seder last night."

"I'll tell you the truth, rabbi," the blacksmith ashamedly replied. "I don't know how to conduct a Seder. So I filled a large goblet with wine and I said: 'Merciful Lord, You're righteous and kind. I'm a poor, ignorant blacksmith. What can you expect from me?' Then I drank the wine, replenished the goblet and kept drinking until I got drunk."

After hearing this succinct recital, Rabbi Levi Isaac said to the blacksmith:

"You observed the festival according to the Jewish spirit. Your humility and penitence are more meritorious than a hundred ceremonies."

ASKING QUESTIONS

The first night of Passover was celebrated within the confines of the immediate family. For the second night, some friends were invited to participate in the *Seder*. When the time came for the ten-year-old son to ask the Four Questions, the boy refused, even though on the previous evening he had chanted them beautifully. Papa kept urging his child to display his ability for the assembled guests but to no avail. The child would not open his mouth.

Finally, the proud Mama said:

"Sonny, if you'll show our guests how smart you are by asking Papa the Four Questions, I'll buy you a nice present."

The boy, most reluctantly and sheepishly, replied:

"Last night when I asked Papa the Four Questions he didn't answer them. I don't want everybody to know how stupid Papa is."

TELL THY SON

Rabbi Levi Isaac of Berditchev, when reciting the *Haggadah,* paused as he read the passage concerning the last of the Four Sons—"He who does not know how to ask." Then he ruminated:

"Who does not know how to ask? He is none other

than myself, Levi Isaac. Master of the Universe, I do not know how to ask You why Your chosen people, the innocent children of Israel, suffer such a long and dreary exile. However, the *Haggadah* commands the father of the son who does not know how to ask questions: 'Reveal to him as it is said (in the Torah): And thou shalt tell to thy son.' O Lord, surely, I am Your child. Now, therefore, reveal to me why my brethren and I endure such suffering."

The Afikoman

The Afikoman, a Greek word meaning dessert, is a piece of Matzah which is put aside at the beginning of the Passover Seder to be eaten at the end of the meal. This is done, some say, to stimulate the participation of the children since they are expected to discover its hiding place and to take possession of it. When the time comes to eat the Afikoman, the children understandably demand a ransom for its return.

THE DISAPPEARING AFIKOMAN

A *Melamed,* who had been engaged to instruct a farmer's son, was invited to remain with the rustic's family for Passover so that he might show them how to prepare for the holiday and how to conduct the traditional *Seder.*

During the *Seder,* at the appropriate time for *Yahatz,* the *Melamed,* in accordance with the established tradition, took the middle one of the three *Matzos* set on the table, broke it in half, put one half back on the dish and the other part, the *Afikoman,* in his pocket.

The farmer, observing this strange action of the *Melamed,* angrily remarked:

"You should be ashamed of yourself! Even though I'm paying you well, I don't begrudge whatever you eat at my table, but you shouldn't steal any *Matzah.*"

PREPARED FOR AN EMERGENCY

The family was celebrating the Passover *Seder* in the traditional manner. When the meal was finished and the father looked for the *Afikoman,* he discovered, as he had naturally expected, that it was missing. He explained to those seated around the festive board that it was not permitted to continue with the service until each one ate a piece of the *Afikoman.*

The youngest child readily admitted that he had taken possession of the special "dessert." Father and son engaged in prolonged negotiations resulting in a promise by the former to give his offspring a bicycle. The boy thereupon yielded the *Afikoman.* Once the father held the prized "dessert" in his hand, he told his son that he would not give him his share of the *Afikoman* unless he was freed of his promise concerning the bicycle.

The boy wasn't the least disturbed. He pulled out of his pocket a piece of the *Afikoman* and crowed:

"See, I kept my share just for such an emergency."

THE REWARD FOR THE AFIKOMAN

Before the start of the *Seder,* the father secretly told each of his four young sons that he would give a reward to the one who would tell him who took the *Afikoman*. He also promised that this reward would be even more valuable than that for the one who held the *Afikoman*.

As each boy was anxious to receive the better reward, no one took the *Afikoman*. And the wise father did not need to give any reward!

THE SHULHAN ARUCH DEVOURED

During the week of Passover, Yossel came to seek the sage advice of Hershele Ostropoler. He had a sad story to relate.

"Now I can understand the harshness of the plagues that Moses brought upon the Egyptians for oppressing the children of Israel. But, Hershele, tell me why should I be so punished? My house is overrun with mice. What's my crime?"

Hershele thoughtfully considered the matter and then suggested:

"Take pieces of the *Afikoman* and place them at the holes where the mice enter. After they eat the *Afikoman*, the mice will be unable to eat anything else."

"Hershele, do the mice know the law that it is forbidden to eat anything after the *Afikoman*?" Yossel asked naïvely.

"It's logical to assume that they know the law," Hershele reassured Yossel. "At my house on the night of the *Seder* the mice devoured the entire *Shulhan Aruch* * so they must be full of the laws and they must know what's permissible and what's forbidden."

* *Shulhan Aruch* is both the meal served at the Passover *Seder* and also the title of the Jewish code of laws.

Too Much Afikoman

During the Passover week, a venerable Jew, who had passed his eightieth birthday, visited a doctor and complained that he felt ill for the first time in his life.

The physician gave him a thorough examination but he was unable to find anything wrong with the octogenarian. He realized, however, that if he would advise the patient that he was in perfect health, it would be most disappointing to him. He finally gave his 'diagnosis':

"You are ill because you ate too much *Afikoman.*"

"How is it possible that I could become sick from eating such a small piece of *Matzah?*" the aged Jew inquired.

"I do not know of a more serious cause of illness," the doctor explained. "A person who has eaten eighty pieces of *Afikoman* must become ill."

The Cup of Elijah

A fifth cup of wine, alluding to the fifth promise of the Lord of a final redemption which Elijah, the prophet of hope and faith, will bring, is called the Cup of Elijah. Towards the end of the Seder, the door is opened to symbolize the welcome of the prophet, a popular figure in Jewish legend.

Prophet or Guest

During the *Seder* service, when Rabbi Menahem Mendel Morgenstern of Kotzk went to open the door to welcome the Prophet Elijah, a guest at his table drank the wine from the cup that had been set aside for Elijah. Returning to the table, the rabbi noticed the prophet's empty cup and a look of embarrassment on the face of his guest.

"My dear friend," Rabbi Mendele said, seeking to ease the conscience of the guest, "both you and Elijah are welcome guests in my home. As the prophet did not appear to drink his wine, you are certainly entitled to it."

A Reincarnated Elijah

As Berel opened the door to extend a hearty welcome to Elijah the Prophet, a fun-loving fellow Helmite chased a goat into his house. The animal jumped upon the *Seder* table and began to wreak havoc with every thing about him.

Berel, certain that the goat was none other than Elijah who had come in response to his invitation, addressed him thus:

"Rabbi Elijah, I beg of you to eat and drink as much as your heart desires but, please, don't do any more damage."

"And the Dog Came . . ."

A gang of rowdies peered through the window of Reb Yankel's house and watched the observance of the *Seder*. When the door was opened to welcome the Prophet Elijah, one of the rowdies dashed into the house, shouting:

"What were you saying?"

Reb Yankel's quick retort caused the rowdy to flee in shame:

"I was reciting *Had Gadya* and I had just said 'And the dog came.' "

A Prisoner's Complaint

A Jewish prisoner complained to a visiting rabbi that the warden did not allow the Jewish inmates to observe their religious laws. Naturally, the rabbi was greatly concerned and asked the prisoner for particulars.

"Two weeks ago when we observed Passover," the inmate related, "the warden arranged a *Seder* for us but he refused to have it conducted properly. When we were reading the *Haggadah* and we were supposed to welcome Elijah the Prophet, the warden didn't let us open the door."

A Handful of Nuts

Joey: Mother, can I have a handful of nuts to play Passover games?

Mother: Of course. Help yourself from the sack.

Joey: I would prefer that you give the nuts to me.

Mother: Why?

Joey: Your hand is bigger than mine.

Obedient Children

Mother: Children, I see that you've again eaten the nuts that I gave you for playing Passover games. I told you that no one should eat his nuts.

Reuben: Mother, no one of us ate his nuts. I gave mine to Simon and he gave me his.

A Slight Exaggeration

"Once I bought a turkey for Passover. It was as large as an elephant. On the eve of Passover the slaughterer killed the fowl. My wife prepared one half of the turkey for the *Seder* to which we invited all of the two hundred families in our town. Everyone enjoyed the turkey. The second half of the turkey we left for the following Passover and until then it laid enough eggs every day to supply all the inhabitants of our town."

More Questions

Why is Passover like an appointment with a good friend?
Because you want to keep it.

Why is the *Haggadah* the same as *Borsht?*
Because they are both read (red).

Why is the door closed when the *Seder* begins?
Because at the start of the *Seder* we read: "Let all who are hungry, enter and eat."

Why are *Matzos* like crackerjacks?
The more you eat, the more you want.

When is stealing rewarded and not punished?
When the *Afikoman* is stolen.

Why are hard-boiled eggs eaten on Passover?

They are a reminder of the Jewish people. The longer eggs are cooked in hot water or roasted on a fire the harder they become. This is also true of Jews.

Why do we have *Haroses* to remind us of the mortar and *Maror* to recall the bitter lives of our ancestors in Egypt but we do not have any reminder of the great wealth which the children of Israel took with them when they left the land of bondage?

The Jews still have some of the mortar and bitterness but they do not have any longer even a faint recollection of the great wealth.

FOLK PROVERBS

Passover is a difficult but a clean festival. (Much labor and money is expended for Passover but it results in a spotlessly clean house.)

He sits as a *Matzah* baker. (One who works only a short time and is idle most of the year.)

He does not mean the *Haggadah* but the *Kneidlach*.

The wise man of the *Haggadah!*

Even the stingiest miser gladly pours a full cup of wine for Elijah the Prophet.

What good is one *Matzah* for a soldier? (This is the complaint of one who receives an insufficient donation.)

The best of the ten plagues are the *Kneidlach*.

Give him what is given on Passover. (Plagues.)

If a piece of the *Afikoman* is stored in the house, the mice will do no damage. (As it is forbidden to eat anything after the *Afikoman*, when the mice eat it, they will be unable to eat anything else.)

SHAVUOS—SEASON OF THE GIVING OF OUR LAW

Receiving the Ten Commandments

CHAPTER EIGHT

SHAVUOS—THE SEASON OF THE GIVING OF OUR LAW

*S*HAVUOS, the Festival of Weeks, or Pentecost (the Greek word for fiftieth) falls on the fiftieth day or seven weeks after the second day of Passover. In the Bible, it is called the Feast of Harvest or Ingathering and the Day of the First Fruits, for in ancient times part of the products of the harvest were joyously offered to God as a reminder that everything belongs to Him and that the peoples of the earth are only His custodians. They are obligated to share with the poor and the stranger the bounties of the Creator.

Besides being an agricultural festival, Shavuos is also the Season of the Giving of Our Law for it was the birthday of Israel's religion, when God gave them the Torah. It is so conceived in our liturgy.

Shavuos has been described by the rabbis as the wedding day of God and Israel, the Torah being the marriage contract. As birthday and wedding day, Shavuos is indeed an auspicious occasion for rejoicing.

Rashi said of Shavuos: "One should rejoice on it by eating and drinking to demonstrate that this day on which the Torah was given is acceptable to him" (Pesahim 68b).

Since the holy Torah is central to Judaism, ample opportunities arose to safeguard its sanctity and to mock the insincerity of its guardians through tales of wit and humor. For we jest most, someone has said, about the things we hold most sacred.

THE MERITS OF THE FESTIVAL

Three Jews were discussing the relative merits of the Three Major Festivals—Passover, Shavuos and Sukkos.

The first one claimed:

"Passover is by far the best of the festivals for we celebrate it with a beautiful *Seder* at which we eat special, delicious foods."

The second Jew held:

"Sukkos is much better than Passover and Shavuos for then we dwell in colorful booths."

The third one contended:

"Shavuos is really far superior to the other festivals. On Passover we are not permitted to eat what we want; on Sukkos we cannot eat where we want; but on Shavuos we may eat what we want, where we want and even when we want."

THE FESTIVAL OF INGATHERING

On the morning of the first day of Shavuos the newly engaged rabbi preached on the significance of the three names of the festival—Season of the Giving of Our Law, Feast of Weeks and Festival of Ingathering. After the services, the rabbi, disturbed at the small attendance in the synagogue, inquired of the president as to the reason for the absence of so many congregants. The president explained the cause of this situation:

"Today happens to be the first of June and the businessmen are occupied in the collection of outstanding bills."

The rabbi then thoughtfully observed:

"It is indeed gratifying to know that, while these Jews do not celebrate Shavuos as the Season of the Giving of our Law or as the Feast of Weeks, they at least observe it as the Festival of Ingathering."

THE GOLDEN CALF

Two *Yeshivah* students were studying the portion of the Torah which recounts that, while Moses tarried on Mount Sinai where he went to receive the Tablets of the Law, Aaron had collected the golden earrings from all the children of Israel and with them he had fashioned a golden calf.

At this point one of the students remarked:

"I do not understand why Aaron made a calf. If he collected so much gold, he should have had more than enough for an ox."

The other promptly countered:

"You should know better! Aaron ordered collectors to amass the golden earrings from the people. It is really a wonder that the collectors turned in enough to make even a calf and not a mouse."

THE WRONG SEASON

A merchant had engaged a coachman to transport a case of dishes to a neighboring town. It was winter.

Snow, slush and ice covered the ground and the roads were dangerously slippery. As a result, the coach reeled into a ditch along the side of the road and the dishes were smashed.

When the coachman returned and reported the accident to the merchant, the latter hailed the unfortunate driver before the rabbi, requesting payment for the breakage. The spiritual leader decreed that the coachman was obligated to pay for the loss in accordance with the laws of the Torah. The poor man bitterly contested this decision. While the rabbi sympathized with him, he felt that it was his duty to uphold Jewish law.

The coachman, seeking to discover a loophole, shrewdly asked the rabbi:

"When was the Torah given?"

"On Shavuos, of course."

"During which season of the year does Shavuos occur?"

"During the summer."

"You see, rabbi," the coachman argued, "that when the Torah was given to the children of Israel it was summer and there was no snow nor ice on the roads. Therefore, the law is understandable. Now, don't you believe that, if the Torah had been given in the winter when the roads are dangerous, the law would not hold me responsible for the damage?"

OUR TORAH

One Shavuos Reb Hayyim was called to the reading of the Torah. As he recited the benediction, "Blessed art Thou, Lord our God, King of the Universe, who hast given unto us the Torah of truth . . . ," he pronounced "unto us" with deep fervor. In reply to the rabbi's inquiry as to the reason that he emphasized that particular phrase, Reb Hayyim explained:

"I am grateful to God that he gave the Torah to the Jews and not to any other people. Can you imagine what would have happened if He had given it to the Russians? They would have punished us for every minute violation of a commandment, even as the Torah decrees. However, we Jews amongst ourselves will always be able to get along."

GIVING AND RECEIVING

The Kotzker rabbi asked:

"Why is Shavuos called the 'Season of the *Giving* of Our Law' and not the 'Season of the *Receiving* of the Law'?"

And then he gave the answer:

"Only on one day—Shavuos—was the Torah given and that was thousands of years ago but it may be received every day. Furthermore, the Torah was given equally to every Jew but every Jew did not receive it equally."

THE PRIORITY OF JUDAISM

A king ordered the Jews and the Karaites of his country to designate representatives to debate in his presence so that he could determine which religion was first established.

The Karaites sent their most learned sage, attired in beautiful garments of silk, while the spokesman for the Jewish community appeared to be a simple man, dressed in every-day clothes.

When the Jewish representative appeared in the throne room of the king, he removed his shoes and held them securely under his arm and thus, barefooted, he approached his royal majesty. The king became exceedingly wroth at this strange behavior. The royal reaction was not unexpected by the Jew who said meekly:

"Your Royal Highness, permit me to explain. When the Jews wish to honor the King of Kings they remove their shoes, as it is written in the Bible: 'Remove thy shoes from thy feet.'"

"But why do you carry the shoes under your arm?" the king was curious to know.

"We learned this practice from a sad experience we once had," the Jew explained. "Before we approached Mount Sinai to receive the Torah, we took off our shoes, but when we returned they were gone. The Karaites had stolen our shoes."

The elegantly clad Karaite spokesman, who was standing by prepared to debate on the subject for which he had been invited, was shocked to hear this false accusation. Unable to restrain himself, he interrupted the conversation between the king and the Jew, shouting:

"That's a lie! When the Torah was given on Mount Sinai there were no Karaites in the world."

"We need go no further, Your Majesty," the Jew casually said. "You heard that even this Karaite admits that the religion of the Jews preceded that of the Karaites."

JEWS LIKE ANIMALS

A: Why is it a custom to eat only dairy foods on Shavuos?

B: There were no animals to slaughter on the first Shavuos as all the *Kosher* animals went to witness the giving of the Law.

A: Apparently the animals followed the example of the Jews. Can we then also assume that the Jews were like animals?

B: That is true. Until the Jews received the Torah they were like animals and only then did they become men. Any Jew who still does not accept the Torah is just like the Israelites before the Holy Law was given to them.

THE UGLY ARE DESPISED

An aged woman appeared before a rabbi and poured forth her tale of woe:

"My husband hates me. He keeps telling me that I'm ugly."

The pious sage, not daring to look at the face of the woman, reluctantly queried:

"Perhaps you are really ugly?"

"I don't know, rabbi," the anguished woman cried. "When my husband married me he called me beautiful. Now, I've become ugly in his sight."

The rabbi attentively followed the argument of the woman. Then he raised his eyes heavenward and said:

"O God, this woman is undoubtedly right. Also we, the children of Israel, have a justifiable complaint against You. When we stood at Mount Sinai You chose us from all the nations. You praised us. And we agreed to accept your contract—the Torah. But now that we have become ugly from many generations of persecution You do not want to save us from our troubles!"

MISSING FROM THE TORAH

One Shavuos a rabbi, discoursing on the festival, said: "If I had been present at Mount Sinai, I would have urged Moses to include in the holy Torah permission for the Jews to do three things so that they would not have to suffer so much.

"First, smoking a cigarette after the *Kugel* on the Sabbath; second, drinking a glass of tea after *Kol Nidrei* on Yom Kippur; and third, bathing after the recital of Lamentations on Tishah B'Av."

The Ten Commandments

On Shavuos, according to tradition, God revealed to Moses on Mount Sinai the Ten Commandments, engraved on two tablets. Since then these commandments have been engraved on the hearts of men and are still the fundamental basis of modern civilization. The sages have indicated that the Ten Commandments in Hebrew consist of 613 letters, the same number as all the commandments in the Torah. The neglect of this supreme code brought sharp reproval from rabbis.

COMMANDMENTS FOR RICH AND POOR

A rabbi who loved his poor congregants had contempt for the wealthy ones. On Shavuos morning, using the Ten Commandments as the theme of his sermon, he told the following story:

"When Moses appeared at the foot of Mount Sinai,

he carried the two tablets on which the Ten Commandments were engraved. The tablets were also studded with precious jewels. As Moses saw the children of Israel worshipping the Golden Calf, he broke the tablets. The rich Jews, who naturally were standing near the leader, immediately hastened to pick up the larger pieces of the tablets so that they might have more of the precious jewels. When they had selected the choicest pieces of the tablets, the poor people who had been in the rear came forward and collected the remaining fragments. It was found that on the large pieces there were engraved the words 'Thou Shalt . . . Murder,' 'Thou shalt . . . commit adultery,' 'Thou shalt . . . steal,' 'Thou shalt . . . bear false witness.' On the small fragments appeared only the word 'not.' That is why the rich are permitted to murder, to steal and to bear false witness while the poor are forbidden to do anything."

VIOLATION OF A COMMANDMENT

On the eve of Shavuos a thief who stole a pair of silver candlesticks was brought before the rabbi. The sage scolded the miscreant:

"Today you should be preparing to receive the Torah. Instead you have violated one of the commandments of the Torah—'Thou shalt not steal.' "

The thief, who did not appear to be ashamed of his crime, replied:

"Believe me, rabbi, I seriously considered what I was doing before I stole the candlesticks. I was faced with a dilemma: either to violate the commandment 'Thou shalt not steal' or 'Thou shalt not covet.' As both commandments are of equal importance, I soon realized that if I would transgress the commandment 'Thou shalt not covet,' I would be a sinner and yet I would have nothing. Now, I have violated only one commandment but, at least, I have the candlesticks."

A Consolation

On Shavuos the rabbi appropriately preached a sermon on the Ten Commandments, enumerating the importance of each. Noah listened attentively and was truly conscience-stricken. After pondering the enormity of his transgressions, he finally consoled himself with a happy thought that struck him:

"At least, I have never made a graven image."

Upholders of the Law

On entering a synagogue in Berlin, a Polish Jew was overwhelmed by the disregard of Jewish traditions that was evident. Noticing the beautiful Ark of the Law upon which were set two tablets with the Ten Commandments supported by two lions, he thought to himself:

"Apparently, the only ones in this congregation who uphold the Ten Commandments are the lions."

"Keep the Commandments . . ."

During the week preceding Shavuos, a rabbi visited a number of the prominent members of his congregation to solicit flowers and plants to adorn the synagogue during the festival.

When he saw one of his members, a *nouveau riche,* and presented his request, the latter, attempting to vaunt both his erudition and his generosity, offered:

"Instead of giving flowers in honor of Shavuos, I will present the synagogue with the tablets of the Ten Commandments."

The rabbi immediately retorted:

"It would be better that you *keep* the commandments and give something else to the synagogue."

Tikkun Shavuos

Tikkun Shavuos, an anthology of excerpts from the Bible and rabbinic literature, is studied throughout the entire first night of the festival as an expression of grateful appreciation for the gift of the Torah.

RECITING TIKKUN SHAVUOS

On the first night of Shavuos, Jews were assembled in the synagogue of the *Magid* of Dubnow, reciting *Tikkun Shavuos*. During the course of the long night, the *Magid* arose to speak:

"Pious Jews need to learn from the practice of business men. They employ salesmen who carry samples of their wares to show customers. When the latter place orders, the salesmen know that they can be filled from the stocks that are in the stores or warehouses of their employers. It is, of course, needless to say that if a salesman displays samples for which there is no stock he must be either a cheat or a fool.

"The same principle applies to the recital of *Tikkun Shavuos*. On this night when we celebrate the season of the giving of the Torah, we take samples from the vast warehouse of Jewish literature and study them. If, however, we do not possess a wider knowledge of Jewish lore, if we are not well-versed in the original source because we have neglected to study the Torah throughout the year, then we are either cheats or fools."

On Being Awake Shavuos Night

A Jew was complaining about the necessity of remaining awake on the first night of Shavuos to recite the *Tikkun*.

"It is really terrible with that night. I slept two nights before and two nights after, and I also fell asleep on Shavuos night, and I am still sleepy."

The Book of Ruth

The Biblical Book of Ruth is read in the synagogue on Shavuos for the acceptance of Judaism by Ruth is comparable to the acceptance of the Torah by the children of Israel. The book is also reminiscent of Shavuos for it describes charmingly the agricultural life of ancient Palestine and how the poor gathered in the harvest gleaning.

The Idyl of Ruth

During the session before Shavuos, a teacher wanted to instruct her Sunday school class in the Book of Ruth so that the pupils would understand the reason it was read on the forthcoming festival.

"Who knows anything about Ruth?" the pedagogue asked.

Joseph unhesitatingly raised his hand and, as the

teacher nodded to him, he said in a firm and clear voice:

"Ruth was the home run king of baseball."

When the laughter subsided, the teacher decided to narrate the story which she did. At the conclusion, desiring to ascertain if her pupils had paid attention, she asked:

"How did Boaz display kindness to Ruth?"

"Boaz ordered the reapers to permit Ruth to gather gleanings from his field," Rose responded correctly.

"Boaz did another kindness for Ruth," the teacher continued. "Can anyone tell me what else he did for her?"

"Married her!" shouted one of the bright pupils.

Blintzes

Dairy dishes characterize the foods eaten on Shavuos. They welcome with due humility the "Season of the Giving of Our Torah." Young children usually do not eat meat; they are too immature for this heavy diet. Similarly, Jews consider themselves too immature in their knowledge of Torah and are reminded of this by the very foodstuffs of this holiday.

Another explanation given of the use of dairy foods on this holiday is that milk and honey are comparable to the nourishment and sweetness of the Torah.

Of all the delectable dairy dishes associated with Shavuos, the supreme delight is Blintzes (rolled pancakes filled with cheese). What people is without stories about its national food?

The Pleasure of Blintzes

Hayyim learned that on Shavuos the well-to-do Jews ate *Blintzes*. While he had always eaten only dairy foods on this festival in accordance with the Jewish custom, he never had this particular delicacy. Anxious to observe the holiday punctiliously, he requested his wife Sarah to make *Blintzes* for Shavuos.

"To make *Blintzes* I need eggs," the spouse replied.

"Make them without eggs," Hayyim suggested.

"Cheese is also needed for *Blintzes*."

"If there is no cheese, we can have *Blintzes* without cheese."

The dutiful wife, anxious to please her husband, made *Blintzes* without eggs and cheese.

When Hayyim returned home from the synagogue on Shavuos night, he recited the festival *Kiddush* and made himself ready to enjoy the *pièce de résistance*. As he ate the *Blintzes,* a look of pain and confusion spread over his face. Turning to Sarah, he said with a deep sigh:

"I fail to see why rich Jews enjoy *Blintzes*."

Blintzes on Shavuos

On the eve of Shavuos, Sammy's mother made the traditional festival dish—*Blintzes*. Sammy was unable to hold out until the evening to partake of this delicacy and stealthily entered the kitchen while his mother was occupied elsewhere and greedily devoured most of the *Blintzes*.

During the festival meal as the mother was ready to serve the *Blintzes,* she was confounded to find that so many had disappeared. She reported the mystery to her husband who quickly surmised that his offspring had already celebrated Shavuos for himself.

Addressing Sammy in a stern voice of reproach, his father said:

"I should spank you for eating the *Blintzes*. However, I'm prepared to forgive you if you can tell me the reason we eat this dish on Shavuos."

Unhesitatingly and with a grin on his face, the precocious youngster replied:

"It's enough reason for me that they're good and I don't think you can find a better reason."

Who's Counting?

After the Shavuos morning services in the synagogue, a kind householder invited a stranger to his home for the festival meal. As was traditional, the hostess served cheese *Blintzes*.

The host, proud of his wife's cooking and especially of the tasty *Blintzes* she made, urged the stranger:

"I see that you too enjoy my wife's *Blintzes*. Help yourself to more."

"Yes, I certainly do love the *Blintzes*," the stranger readily admitted. "However, I don't want to deprive you of any more as I've already had six."

"So you've already eaten eight," the host reminded his guest, "but who's counting?"

The Ten Commandments of Helm

In the city of Helm there dwelled Lemech, a teacher, and his wife Leah, a peddler. Both were advanced in years. Both worked hard and together eked out the bare necessities of life. The Passover festival had passed and their thoughts naturally turned to the next holiday— Shavuos.

Lemech said to Leah:

"Leah, although God has granted me a lengthy and full life, I've never eaten *Blintzes* on Shavuos. Do you think we can do anything about filling this obvious void?"

Leah was most sympathetic to the need of overcoming this lack which she, too, had experienced. Possessed of as much wisdom as her husband, the teacher in Israel, she proposed a unique scheme to enable them to realize their ambition of eating *Blintzes* on Shavuos.

"Listen to me, Lemech," she said. "Let's take the large trunk with wheels that my parents gave us as part of my dowry. We'll make two small holes in it, one at each end. Every evening I'll insert a coin from my earnings in one hole and you'll do likewise in the other hole. On the eve of Shavuos we'll open the trunk, take out the money and use it to buy what is required to make *Blintzes*."

Lemech was joyfully amazed at the ingenuity of his wife and readily agreed to adopt her plan. No sacrifice would be too great for the sake of eating *Blintzes* on Shavuos!

On the first evening that the couple were to initiate their self-imposed savings plan, Leah took out a coin to insert in the trunk. As she was about to do so, a brilliant stroke of genius smote her. She thought to herself:

"I need my meager earnings to buy food for our daily sustenance. Let Lemech save his money for the *Blintzes!*"

When Lemech arrived home, he promptly approached

the trunk with the good and sincere intention of putting in a coin. Removing the money from his pocket, he was about to drop it into the trunk when his hand suddenly became paralyzed, as if an angel were holding it fast, and this warning was revealed to his inner consciousness:

"Lemech, you, as a teacher in Helm, are engaged in a holy occupation. Let not your sacred earnings be used for such mundane matters as *Blintzes*. Let Leah save from the money she earns by peddling earthly wares."

Let the truth be told! Lemech did not require much coaxing and he accepted the chiding of the hidden voice that called to him.

The eve of Shavuos arrived. Leah brought forth the key to the trunk and, in the presence of Lemech, with adequate preliminary fanfare, she inserted it in the lock and turned it. Graciously, she gave the honor of raising the cover of the trunk to her beloved husband. In great anticipation, Lemech laid both hands on the cover and, with a prayer in his heart, raised it.

First, Leah looked in the trunk. Second, Lemech looked in the trunk. Then, both together, they looked at the emptiness of the trunk. Leah looked at Lemech; Lemech looked at Leah. They looked at each other. But not for long!

She grabbed his beard. He grabbed her hair. She pulled. He pulled. She screamed. He screamed.

Leah and Lemech screamed so that their voices were heard throughout the streets of Helm. This commotion failed to interfere with the people of Helm who were deeply engrossed in the preparations for Shavuos. Anyway, screaming was a favorite method of the Helmites to win an argument and its frequent use never disturbed the populace.

Pulling each other before the open trunk, Leah and Lemech lost their balance and fell, head over heels, into the empty trunk. This sudden movement brought down the cover into its place and closed in the couple.

The vibrations caused by the still struggling pair speeded the trunk on its wheels through the open door, that was without a threshold, down the steep hill, at the foot of which was the synagogue. The trunk wended its way to the house of worship whose doors were always open. With a complete lack of deference for the holy place, the trunk rode on into the synagogue and came to a halt only when the impact, physical rather than spiritual, of the Holy Ark faced it.

The rabbi, the sexton and the trustees, assembled in the synagogue to decorate it with greens in honor of Shavuos, were horror-struck at the sight of the trunk that did not fear to stand, defiantly, before the Holy Ark. It did not take long for the rabbi and the trustees to arrive at a brave decision. They courageously ordered the sexton to open the trunk so that they might see what had been sent to them from on high for Shavuos. The sexton girded himself with *Tephilin* and *Talis,* recited the prayers of confession before death, and, with *Shema Yisrael* on his lips, opened the trunk.

The synagogue dignitaries were astounded to look upon Lemech and Leah, completely exhausted and barely conscious. After helping the couple get out of the trunk, they queried them. Learning what had happened, the rabbi and the trustees promptly decided to promulgate rules and regulations to avoid similar occurrences in the future.

The following morning at the Shavuos services, after the Ten Commandments were read in the Torah, the rabbi read another set of ten commandments that are a heritage of the Jews of Helm for all generations.

And the rabbi spoke all these words, saying:

1. I am the rabbi of Helm, who brought thee out of the lands of wisdom, out of the houses of learning.

2. Thou shalt have no other rabbis before me.

3. Remember the days of Shavuos, to keep them holy.

4. Honor thy husband or thy wife, that thy days may be long in the city of Helm.

5. Thou shalt not pull hair, neither the hair of a head nor the hair of a face.

6. Thou shalt not make unto thee a trunk with wheels.

7. Thou shalt place thresholds on thy doors.

8. Thou shalt keep the doors of the synagogue closed.

9. Thou shalt not save money.

10. Thou shalt not covet *Blintzes*, neither for Shavuos, nor any festival, nor any day; thou shalt not covet *Blintzes* of cheese, nor of potatoes, nor of any thing which is good to eat.

FOLK PROVERBS

Hol Ha-Moed Shavuos!

The Torah of Moses and the jealousy of women are eternal!

It is as true as the Law of Moses. (To indicate that one is telling a lie, it is said: "It is as true as the Law of Lokshun.")

DAYS OF FASTING

Reading Lamentations

CHAPTER NINE

DAYS OF FASTING

*F*AST *days, with the exception of the Day of Atonement, occupy a relatively minor place in the Jewish
calendar. These days recall some of the grievous calami-
ties that befell the Jews throughout their variegated
history.*

*Four fast days—occurring on the Third of Tishri,
the Seventeenth of Tamuz, the Tenth of Teves and the
Ninth of Av—are associated with the destruction of the
Temple. The first eight days of Av are observed as a
period of mourning prior to the fast. The Fast of Esther
recalls the three days of fasting by the Jewish queen before she appeared in the presence of the king on behalf
of her people in Persia.*

*That fasting and gloom, although sometimes neces-
sary to stir the historic consciousness of a people, are
foreign to the joyous spirit of Judaism may be deduced
from the words of Rabbi Abraham Joshua Heshel of
Apta: "If I had the authority, I would abolish all the
fast days except Tishah B'Av and Yom Kippur. There
never is any problem with these two fast days. Who is
able to eat on the day when the Temple was destroyed*

and who would want to eat on the sacred Day of Atonement?"

How then can wit and humor find a place on these sad occasions? Not directly, but indirectly through the weaknesses of men. For Jews, as for all humans, hypocrisy is a besetting sin. And so, those who would "cut corners" or in some way indulge their weaknesses became the butt and target of the Jew's sense of righteous wit and blunt humor.

EATING WHILE FASTING

A *Hasid* and a *Misnagid* were engaged in a heated discussion of the virtues of the Hasidic rabbi.

The *Hasid,* lauding his rabbi in the highest terms, boasted:

"The rabbi, God bless him, fasts every day except on Sabbaths and festivals."

The *Misnagid* sneeringly retorted:

"I myself saw your rabbi eating and drinking on a weekday."

The *Hasid* undauntingly replied:

"You are a fool! You fail to understand even simple matters. The rabbi purposely eats and drinks on weekdays so that no one should suspect that he is fasting."

A PUBLIC FAST DAY ABOLISHED

Rabbi Abraham Joshua Heshel of Apta was opposed to the self-castigators who frequently imposed upon themselves days of fasting. One day, arriving in a village, he was informed that a public fast day had been proclaimed so that the Jews might devote themselves to praying for rain to relieve a severe drought that had brought thirst and famine in its wake.

Rabbi Abraham Joshua immediately went to a public inn which was owned by a pious Jew, seated himself comfortably and ordered a sumptuous meal. The inn-keeper, who recognized the distinguished spiritual leader, was aghast. Hesitatingly, he reproved the rabbi with this mild rebuke:

"To-day is a public fast day!"

"I'm aware of it yet I want the meal to be served," ordered the rabbi. "I must set an example for the fools in this village. Why are you fasting? Is it because you require rain that will assure you of water to drink and food to eat? If you fast, the result will be the opposite of what you seek. God will see that you do not require water and food to exist. Now, go and tell all the Jews to eat and drink so that the Almighty will understand your needs and He will cause rain to fall."

Fasting by Proxy

The sexton of a synagogue was engaged by the *Gabbai*, a conscientious Jew, to fast on his behalf on the Fast Day of Gedaliah. During the middle of that afternoon, the *Gabbai* decided to visit the sexton to see how he was faring. Entering the latter's home, he was outraged upon seeing the sexton generously feeding himself. In a fit of righteous indignation, he shouted:

"You reprobate! How dare you eat? I paid you well to fast for me!"

"Please, be seated and I'll explain to you what happened," the sexton courteously said. "The president of the synagogue also hired me to fast for him today.

However, I'm not too strong and it's really impossible for me to fast for both of you. Now, I'll tell you what I decided to do. I hate the president as he makes my life miserable so I made up my mind not to fast for him. But I'm still fasting for you and I'm eating only for the president."

On the Fast of Gedaliah

A Jewish scoffer was asked why he did not fast on the Fast Day of Gedaliah. He gave four reasons:

"First, if Gedaliah had not been killed then, he would be dead by now anyway. Second, if I would be killed, I doubt that anyone would fast on the anniversary of my death. Third, if I'm hungry, I cannot fast. Fourth, and last but not least, if I don't fast on the Day of Atonement, why should I observe such a minor fast day?"

On the Fast of Esther

It was the Fast of Esther. The rabbi was seated in his dining room enjoying a hearty luncheon. Suddenly the door opened and a Jew entered unannounced. The latter was flabbergasted to witness this flagrant violation of the fast day by the rabbi. However, the sight gave him courage to ask his spiritual leader a question, which was the purpose of his visit anyway.

"Rabbi, I'm not feeling well today and I want to know if it's permissible for me to eat."

The rabbi, without interrupting his meal, replied in a shocked tone:

"I'm amazed that you even ask such a question. You should know that you must fast."

"But, rabbi, I can't understand. You yourself aren't fasting and yet you forbid me to eat."

"I'm wiser than you," the sage retorted with a grin on his lips and a mouth full of food. "I did not ask a rabbi if I may eat."

ON THE FAST OF TAMUZ 17

When Rabbi Naphtali Tzvi Yehudah Berlin of Wolozin was advanced in years and his physical strength had ebbed away, he nevertheless insisted on fasting on the Seventeenth Day of Tamuz, even though his doctor had urged him to eat. One year on this fast day, the rabbi had several guests in his home who were not particularly meticulous in their observance of Jewish traditions. About noon they complained to the rabbi that they lacked sufficient strength to continue fasting. Without hesitation, the sage asked his wife to bring food for the guests and he himself served them, although he did not touch a morsel. His sexton observed these strange proceedings in utter amazement. Noticing the reproving look on the face of the sexton, the rabbi whispered in his ear:

"A public fast does not take precedence over the reception of guests."

EATING OF MEAT PERMITTED

During the first nine days of the month of Av, when it is forbidden to eat meat as a sign of mourning, an emaciated and sickly child appeared before Rabbi Hayyim of Brisk. The child said:

"My mother asked if I'm permitted to eat meat during the nine days."

The discerning rabbi gently replied:

"My son, tell your mother that not only is it permitted for you to eat meat but she may also eat meat during the nine days."

The rabbi's followers who heard this exceptionally lenient decision were amazed. When the child departed, Rabbi Hayyim explained:

"You shouldn't wonder about my decision. A pale and sick child is evidence that his mother is also sickly and requires adequate nourishment."

EATING OF MEAT REQUIRED

During the year of a severe drought, the *Parnasim* in Lodz decided to save food by not feeding the children of the Talmud Torah any meat during the first nine days of Av. Thus, they would incidentally also observe a tradition. Learning of this decision, Rabbi Elijah Hayyim summoned the *Parnasim* and asked them:

"Aren't you aware that it is definitely forbidden to feed the school children the food that you are giving them during the Nine Days of Av?"

With righteous self-satisfaction, they replied:

"God forbid that we should transgress a Jewish custom. We have already arranged not to feed the children any meat."

"You misunderstand my question," the rabbi explained. "It is the dairy foods which the children are forbidden to eat. They are young and the study of the

Torah saps whatever strength they may have. Therefore, they require meat and it is your duty to give it to
them."

HERSHELE COMPLIES WITH THE LAW

During the Nine Days of Av Hershele Ostropoler was
seen eating meat. A fellow-townsman approached him
and unhesitatingly asked:

"Hershele, don't you know that during the Nine Days
a Jew should eat only dairy foods?"

"One doesn't show a fool an unfinished job," Hershele responded indignantly and sarcastically. "If you'll
wait a couple of minutes, you'll see that I'll eat cheese
with cream."

CONCLUSIVE PROOF

One Tishah B'Av afternoon, Yossel dragged Shlomo
into the rabbi's house.

"Rabbi," Yossel protested, "I saw Shlomo eating just
now and . . ."

"If what he says is true," Shlomo interrupted, "let
him tell you what I was eating."

"Lamb chops!" Yossel testified.

Thereupon Shlomo pulled out of his coat pocket a
piece of cheese and started to eat it, saying:

"I ask you, rabbi, would I eat cheese now without
waiting six hours after eating meat?"

EATING FOR A CURE

On Tishah B'Av a rabbi passed a restaurant and
noticed one of his congregants seated inside and eating.

He hastily entered the eating place and severely berated the violator of the fast day. The latter sought to justify his action, saying:

"I am not eating for pleasure but only for a cure."

The rabbi carefully looked at the Jew and became convinced that he was really perfectly healthy. He said to him:

"It's truly commendable that you follow the ways of the Almighty. You must know that He always sends the cure before the illness. You're apparently taking a cure before you have an illness. Now that you have taken a cure, you'll inevitably get an illness."

AN EXCELLENT HIDING PLACE

Shmerel was not amenable to fasting on Tishah B'Av. Therefore, on the eve of the fast day, while his wife was out of the kitchen, he took bread and herring and hid the food so that he would be able to satisfy his appetite the following day. It did not take long for his God-fearing wife to notice that some food was missing. Suspecting what Shmerel had done, she was apprehensive lest he be duly punished. She carefully searched for the missing food in the pantry, the cellar, the attic and in every other conceivable hiding place. Yet she failed to discover the bread and the herring. Hastening to the rabbi, she exposed the plot of her husband.

The rabbi summoned Shmerel and demanded that he reveal the hiding place.

Fearful of the rabbi's wrath, Shmerel sheepishly admitted:

"I found an excellent hiding place—in the Passover dishes."

A Hearty Appetite!

Israel Lipkin Salanter was informed that a party was taking place on the night of Tishah B'Av at the home of one of the town's intelligentsia. Fully aware that the feast was intentionally designed to desecrate the fast day, the sage decided to visit the celebrants.

Opening the door of the home where the feast was taking place, the rabbi entered and greeted the assemblage.

"A hearty appetite to all of you!" he bid them.

Despite their sacrilegious designs, the celebrants felt ashamed that the venerated rabbi should find them feasting when they should be fasting. Furthermore, they were unable to fathom the meaning of the rabbi's greeting.

Observing the amazement revealed in their faces, the rabbi explained:

"I wished you 'a hearty appetite' so that your eating on Tishah B'Av will not be with the intention of violating the fast but rather because you have hearty appetites which make you ill from hunger and thus you may be exempt from fasting."

An Incurable Illness

An old Jewish woman paid a visit to a famous Vienna professor of medicine and complained of pains in her stomach. The professor gave her a thorough examination and was unable to diagnose the cause of her complaint. Finally, he asked the patient:

"Since when have you been feeling these pains?"

"Since Tishah B'Av."

"What is Tishah B'Av?" the professor inquired.

"The day that the Temple in Jerusalem was destroyed."

"And when did that occur?"

"Nearly two thousand years ago," the enlightened woman explained.

Hearing this explanation, the professor indignantly protested:

"Even I can't cure a sickness that's two thousand years old!"

LAMENTATIONS

An author approached a prominent rabbi with the request for an endorsement of a commentary that he had written on the Book of Lamentations. He told the sage that if Jews would study his commentary on Tishah B'Av, when it is customary to read the Book of Lamentations, they would be really mournful.

The rabbi perused the commentary for a few minutes and, finding it quite unintelligible, said:

"I agree with you that, if Jews would study your commentary on Lamentations, it would sadden them. Nevertheless, I suggest that you now write lamentations on the commentary."

REJOICING ON TISHAH B'AV

When asked why he rejoiced on Tishah B'Av, a traditional day for fasting and mourning, Joseph explained:

"If on Purim, when only two verses of the Scroll [of Esther] are read to the sad and poignant tune of the Scroll of Lamentations, we are enjoined to be merry,

then on Tishah B'Av when the entire Scroll [of La-
mentations] is read mournfully, we should be exceedingly joyous."

Taking a Family Stroll

When can a poor man take a stroll with his wife and
children?

Only on two days during the year—Yom Kippur and
Tishah B'Av.

Why only on these days?

It is well known that a poor man never has enough
shoes for all the members of his family so that not all
of them can leave their house at the same time. However, they can all go out on Yom Kippur and Tishah
B'Av since it is not permitted to wear shoes on those
days.

Folk Proverbs

Tishah B'Av pervaded the house.

What is a Jewish pleasure? A cool Tishah B'Av.

By fasting one does not save food. (After the fast he
eats more than usual.)

There are three pairs of fast days: Man and wife
(Fast of Gedaliah and Fast of Esther), a long and a short
one (Seventeenth of Tamuz and Tenth of Teves), and
a black and a white one (Tishah B'Av and Yom Kippur).

SEASONS OF GLADNESS

Ceremony of Separation

CHAPTER TEN

SEASONS OF GLADNESS

AN INDIGNANT COMPLAINT

A Jew complained indignantly to the Almighty:
"Why do You mock us? If the children of Israel, Your
chosen people, want to enjoy the festival of Passover,
You don't allow them to eat what they want; if they
want to satiate themselves on Shavuos, You don't per
mit them to eat meat; if they want to be comfortable on
Sukkos, You forbid them to dwell in their own homes;
if they want to rejoice on Rosh Hashanah, You arouse
their fears with the blowing of the *Shofar;* if they want
to observe Yom Kippur by prayer, charity and repentance, You exhaust their strength by making them fast;
and if they want to have true pleasure on the Sabbath,
You refuse them the delight of smoking."

DIFFICULT SEASONS

Spring and summer are the most difficult seasons for
Jews. For seven weeks, from Passover to Shavuos, they
count and sigh; for three weeks, from the Seventeenth
Day of Tamuz to Tishah B'Av, they mourn and sigh;
for the four weeks of the month of Elul, they blow the

Shofar and sigh; and, during the rest of the weeks, they sweat and sigh.

A Bar Mitzvah Speech

The thirteen-year-old lad was delivering his *Bar Mitzvah* speech. Although he began his oration rather eloquently, he suddenly became flustered and concluded with these fervent promises:

"I promise to be a good Jew, to fulfill all the commandments of the Torah and to observe all the Jewish holidays. I promise to fast on Purim, to feast on Yom Kippur, to visit the *Sukkah* on Shavuos, to light candles on the eight days of Passover and to eat *Matzos* on Hanukkah."

A Jack of All Trades

A Jew is a jack of all trades:
  a *Matzah* baker on Passover.
  a general on Lag Ba-Omer.
  a gardener on Shavuos.
  a *Shofar* blower on Rosh Hashanah.
  a faster on Yom Kippur.
  a builder on Sukkos.
  a *Dreidel* maker on Hanukkah.
  a *Shalah Monos* carrier on Purim.

From Saratoga Springs

Morris Ginsberg, who was taking the baths at Saratoga Springs, wrote to his wife:

"Every morning we rise early as we do for *Selihos;* we wear our best clothes as we do on Passover; we fast as we do on Tishah B'Av; and we go to the waters as we do on Rosh Hashanah."

THE RICH MAN'S CONTRIBUTION

The rich man's miserly contribution to the charity fund was—
    like a *Lulav* without an *Esrog*
    like a cup without wine
    like candlesticks without candles
    like *Hamantashen* without *Mohn*
    like *Blintzes* without cheese.

IN AN IMMIGRANT CAMP

Conditions in an immigrants' camp in Israel were compared to the Jewish holidays. The newcomers were dressed in torn clothes as on Purim; they were hungry as on Yom Kippur; and they lived in leaking huts as on Sukkos.

STRANGE CUSTOMS

Mary O'Brien, a maid in a Jewish household, was discussing her employers with a friend:
"They are very devout Jews but they have strange customs which I don't understand. On Saturday they eat in the dining room and then the men take turns going into the bathroom where they smoke; on the Ninth Day of the Hebrew month of Av, they smoke in the

dining room and eat in the bathroom; and on the **Day** of Atonement, they both eat and smoke in the bathroom."

A Duty to Eat

Why is *Maos Hittim* collected to provide food for the poor for Passover and not for Sukkos which is also an important festival?

Concerning Passover, it is written in the Bible: "Seven days thou shalt eat *Matzos*." Because it is a duty to eat *Matzos,* provision must also be made for the poor. Concerning Sukkos, it is written: "Seven days thou shalt dwell in booths." It is a duty to dwell in booths on Sukkos but it is not a duty to eat.

Thrice Kreplach

Why are *Kreplach* eaten on Purim, on the eve of Yom Kippur and on Hoshanna Rabbah?

The answer is really simple. *Kreplach* are eaten whenever there is beating. On Purim Haman is beaten, on the eve of Yom Kippur *Kaparos* are beaten and on Hoshanna Rabbah the willows are beaten. Therefore, on these days we eat *Kreplach* which are filled with chopped meat.

The Indifferent Turkey

What difference does it make to the turkey if he is slaughtered for the Purim feast or for the **Passover** *Seder?*

THE THEORY OF RELATIVITY

A group of *Hasidim* had heard of Einstein's theory of relativity. Although several offered various explanations of the theory, they realized that they were really unable to fathom this matter. Finally one of the *Hasidim* arose and expounded:

"Relativity is truly a simple matter. It deals with two matters that are identical and yet are not identical. Let me give you an example. From Minsk to Pinsk the trip takes three hours and from Pinsk to Minsk it takes three hours. However, from Purim to Passover is one month, while from Passover to Purim is eleven months."

A LONG CLIMB

An elderly Jew returned for a visit to his home town in Lithuania after having been in America many years. His former neighbors came to hear him tell of the wonders of the "Golden Land." Describing the New York skyscrapers and apartment houses that reach to the heavens, the visitor told his gaping audience:

"Once I was invited to a Purim *Seudah* at the home of a friend. Although I came to his apartment house on the morning of Purim, until I climbed the numerous flights of stairs and reached his apartment, I found that my friend was conducting a Passover *Seder*."

PHARAOH AND HAMAN

In the warmer regions of eternity, Pharaoh and Haman chanced to meet and engaged in a conversation. Haman said:

"Your Majesty, I have always harbored a complaint against you. You surely understand that I did not have as much authority and power as you possessed, for I was subject to a foolish king. However, you reigned supremely. Hence, I am amazed that you failed to execute your plans to destroy the Jews. Furthermore, it is on account of you that the Jews now celebrate a holiday for eight days."

To this complaint, Pharaoh replied:

"Haman, you are indeed naïve. It is because of you that the Jews observe Purim as a festival of feasting and joy. On the other hand, I am the one who succeeded with the Jews. While it is true that they observe Passover for eight days, it is a heavy burden for them. Even though they exhaust their energy and money in preparation for the holiday, they still do not have sufficient to eat on those days. Moreover, they usually become ill from too much wine, *Matzos* and nuts."

A NEW HOLIDAY

It is told that Adolf Hitler was very superstitious and that he never lost an opportunity to consult astrologers. On one occasion a distinguished astrologer visited Der Fuehrer who asked:

"Tell me the day on which I will die."

Unprepared for such an inquiry, the astrologer resorted to his charts and maps. After due deliberation, he prophesied:

"The signs portend that you will ascend heavenward on a Jewish holiday."

Hitler was dissatisfied with such a vague reply and demanded:

"You must tell me which holiday it will be and when that holiday falls."

This the astrologer was unable to do; however, he reassured Hitler:

"Any day on which you die will be a Jewish holiday."

ALL HOLIDAYS OBSERVED

It is gratifying that all the Jewish holidays are observed properly. The rich Jews observe the feasts and the poor Jews observe the fasts.

GLOSSARY

AFIKOMAN (Dessert)—A piece of *Matzah* put aside at the beginning of the Passover *Seder* which is eaten at the end of the meal.

APIKORUS—Heretic or free-thinker.

BES HA-MIDRASH—House of Study; usually a synagogue.

BIMAH—Pulpit.

BLINTZES—Rolled pancakes filled with cheese; a favorite dish on Shavuos.

DAY OF ATONEMENT—The culmination of the penitential days; the most sacred day in the Jewish year.

DREIDEL (Trendel)—A spinning top used on Hanukkah.

ELIJAH—The prophet of hope and faith.

ESROG—A citron used on Sukkos.

FAST DAY OF GEDALIAH—A day commemorating the assassination of Gedaliah, governor of Palestine after the First Temple was destroyed.

FAST OF ESTHER—Observed the day before Purim, it commemorates the three days of fasting by Esther.

FOUR SONS—The *Haggadah* expounds on four different types of sons.

FOUR QUESTIONS—Questions related to the distinctive character of Passover which are asked by the youngest child at the *Seder*.

GAON—A title given to a genius.

GUT SHABBOS (Good Sabbath)—A greeting for the Sabbath.

HAD GADYA (One Kid)—A song sung at the Passover *Seder*.

HAGGADAH (Narration)—A special book read at the Passover *Seder*.

HALLAH—A twisted loaf of white bread especially prepared for the Sabbath.

HAMANTASHEN—Triangular-shaped cakes filled with poppy seeds eaten on Purim.

HAMETZ—Leavened bread and food, as well as all dishes and cooking utensils used throughout the year, whose use is forbidden on Passover.

HA-NEROS HALOLU (These candles)—A hymn sung following the lighting of the Hanukkah candles.

HANUKKAH (Dedication)—Festival of Dedication, commemorating the rededication of the Temple in Jerusalem after the victory of the Maccabees over the Syrians; also called the Feast of Maccabees.

HAROSES—A dish eaten at the Passover *Seder* as a reminder of the brick and mortar used by the enslaved Israelites in Egypt.

HASAN BERESHIS (Bridegroom of Genesis)—A man who is honored on Simhas Torah by being called up to recite the blessings for the beginning of the reading of the Torah.

HASID—A member of a sect of pietists.

HASIDIM—Plural of *Hasid*.

HASKALAH (Enlightenment)—A Jewish movement in Russia during the nineteenth century.

HAVDALAH (Separation)—On Saturday evening a division is made between Sabbath and weekday by a special ceremony in which blessings are recited over a cup of wine, a braided candle and a spice box.

HELM—A legendary town of many hair-raising and amusing incidents, renowned for its "wise men."

HIGH HOLY DAYS—The New Year and Day of Atonement.

HOSHANNA—A branch of willow used on Hoshanna Rabbah.

HOSHANNA RABBAH—The seventh day of Sukkos.

KADDISH—Mourner's prayer.

KAPAROS—A symbolic ceremony, reminiscent of the offering of a sacrifice, in which charity is given on the eve of the Day of Atonement.

KEYLITSH—A large, braided loaf of white bread with raisins eaten at the Purim *Seudah*.

KIBBUTZ—A cooperative settlement.

KIDDUSH (Sanctification)—A prayer sanctifying the Sabbaths and festivals usually chanted over wine, both evening and morning.

KNEIDLACH—Dumplings eaten on Passover.

KOL NIDREI (All vows)—A solemn prayer chanted before the evening service of Yom Kippur.

KOSHER—Ritually fit for use.

KREPLACH—Triangular-shaped dumplings filled with meat.

KUGEL—A pudding eaten on the Sabbath.

LAG BA-OMER (Thirty-third day in the counting of the Omer)—A minor festival commemorating the bravery of Bar Kochba and Rabbi Akiva.

LATKES—Potato pancakes; the special dish associated with Hanukkah.

LE-HAYYIM (To life)—A toast.

LULAV—Palm branch used on Sukkos.

MAGID—A preacher.

MAHZOR—A festival prayer book.

MAOS HITTIM (Wheat money)—Funds to meet the Passover needs of the poor.

MASKIL—An enlightened person.

MASMID—A diligent student.

MATZAH—Unleavened bread eaten during Passover.

MATZOS—Plural of *Matzah*.

MEGILLAH (Scroll)—Usually refers to the Scroll of Esther, the story of Purim.

MELAMED—Teacher.

MEZUZAH—A religious symbol attached to a doorpost containing Biblical verses written on parchment.

MINYAN—Quorum of ten male Jews required for public worship services.

MI SHE-BARACH—A prayer offered on behalf of each person called to the reading of the Torah.

MISHLOAH MONOS (Sending of portions)—The tradition of sending gifts on Purim.

MISNAGID—An opponent of the Hasidic movement.

MITZVAH—A commandment; a good deed.

NEILAH (Closing)—The final service of Yom Kippur.

NESHAMAH YESERAH—An extra soul which the Jew who observes the Sabbath receives.

NINE DAYS OF AV—The days observed as a period of mourning.

PARNAS—A communal leader or officer of a congregation.

PASSOVER—Festival commemorating the exodus from Egypt.

PITMA—Pestlelike protuberance of *Esrog*.

PURIM (Lots)—The Feast of Lots; also called the Feast of Esther.

REBBETZIN—Wife of a rabbi.

ROSH HASHANAH (Head of the year)—The Jewish New Year.

SABBATH—The seventh day of the week; the day of rest.

SABBATH OF REPENTANCE—The Sabbath that falls between Rosh Hashanah and Yom Kippur.

SEDER (Order)—The order of the service in the home on the first two nights of Passover.

SELIHOS—Penitential prayers recited during the season of the High Holy Days, sometimes between midnight and dawn.

SEUDAH (Meal)—A festive meal at the conclusion of Purim.

SEVENTEENTH DAY OF TAMUZ—A day of fasting to commemorate the breach made by Nebuhadnezzar in the walls surrounding Jerusalem.

SHABBOS GOY (Sabbath Gentile)—A Gentile who does such things as kindling the light and making fires for Jews on Saturday.

SHABBOS HA-GADOL (The Great Sabbath)—The Sabbath which falls before Passover.

SHALAH MONOS—See *Mishloah Monos*.

SHALAH MONOS TREGGERS—Messengers who carry Purim gifts.

SHAMASH—Sexton or servant.

SHAVUOS—The Festival of Pentecost or Weeks; also the Season of the Giving of Our Law and Festival of the First Fruits.

SHEMA YISRAEL (Hear O Israel)—Israel's confession of faith.

SHEMINI ATZERES—The Eighth Day of Solemn Assembly which follows Sukkos.

SHOFAR (Trumpet)—A ram's horn blown during the month of Elul and on the High Holy Days.

SHOHET—Ritual slaughterer.

SHOLOM ALEICHEM (Peace unto you)—A hymn sung in the home on Friday evening; also a greeting.

SHULHAN ARUCH (Prepared table)—The meal served at the Passover *Seder* and the title of the Jewish code of law.

SHUSHAN PURIM—The day following Purim. The holiday was celebrated on this day in Shushan as final triumph was achieved in that city then.

SIMHAS TORAH—The day of Rejoicing in the Law.

SIYUM (Completion)—The completion of the study of a tractate of the Talmud.

STREIMEL—A fur-trimmed hat worn by Hasidim.

SUKKAH—A booth or tabernacle.

SUKKOS—The Festival of Booths or Tabernacles.

TALIS—A prayer shawl.

TASHLICH (Casting)—A ceremony symbolising the casting away of sins into the depths of the waters.

TEPHILLIN—Phylacteries.

TIKKUN SHAVUOS—A collection of excerpts from the Bible and rabbinic literature studied during the first night of Shavuos.

TISHAH B'AV (Ninth Day of Av)—A fast day in commemoration of the destruction of the Temple.

TORAH—Law; Pentateuch.

YESHIVAH—A Talmudical academy.

YAHATZ—The breaking of the middle cake of *Matzah* of which one piece is put away for the *Afikoman*.

YOM KIPPUR—Day of Atonement.

SELECTED BIBLIOGRAPHY

Agnon, Samuel Joseph, *Days of Awe*. New York, Schocken Books, 1948.

Ariel, Z., *Hahamim Ve-Tipshim*. Tel Aviv, Joseph Sreberek, 1950.

Aschkenasy, Isaac, *Otzros fun Yiddishen Humor*. New York, Tel Aviv, 1929.

Ausubel, Nathan, *A Treasury of Jewish Folklore*. New York, Crown Publishers, 1948; *A Treasury of Jewish Humor*. New York, Doubleday & Co., 1951.

Ben Mordecai, *Helmer Naranim*. New York, Hebrew Publishing Co., 1929.

Bernstein, Ignatz, *Yiddishe Sprichworter un Redensarten*. Warsaw, 1908.

Bloch Chayim, *Das Jüdische Volk in seiner Anekdote*. Berlin, Verlag fun kulturpolitik, 1931.

Bostamsky, S., *Beim Kval*. Wilna, Di Neie Yiddishe Folkshul, 1920.

Davidson, Efraim, *Sehok Penu*. Tel Aviv, Matmonim, 1951.

Druyanov, Alter, *Sefer Ha-Bedihah Ve-ha-Hidud*. Frankfurt, 1921–22.

Eizbitz, Israel, *Der Lustiger Hoiz Freund*. Rochester, New York, 1919.

Fishman, Yehudah Leib Hakohen, *Hagim U-Moadim*. Jerusalem, Mosad Harav Kook, 1944.

Goodman, Philip, *The Purim Anthology*. Philadelphia, Jewish Publication Society of America, 1949.

Grossman, William, *Jewish Humor*. Passaic, N.J., Columbia Press, 1940.

Heilperin, Falk, *Helem Va-Hahamehah*. Tel Aviv, Jezreal, 1939; *Hakme Helem*. Tel Aviv, Jezrael, n.d.

Learsi, Rufus, *The Book of Jewish Humor*. New York, Bloch Publishing Co., 1941.

Lehrman, S. M., *The Jewish Festivals*. London, Shapiro, Vallentine & Co., 1938.

Libowitz, Nehemiah S., *Ha-Shomea Yitzhak*. New York, 1906; *Sepher Shashuim*. New York, Bloch Publishing Co., 1927.

Lipson, M., *Anshe Midot*. Tel Aviv, Dvir. 1, 1927. 2, 1927. 3, 1928. 4, 1934; *Di Velt Dertselt*. New York, Dorot, 1928. 2 vols.; *Mi-Dor Dor*. Tel Aviv–New York, Dorot, 1929–1938. 3 vols.

Litwin, A., *Likvod Pesah*. New York, 1938.

Mendelsohn, S. Felix, *Here's A Good One: Stories of Jewish Wit and Wisdom*. New York, Bloch Publishing Co., 1947; *The Jew Laughs*. Chicago, L. M. Stein, 1935; *Let Laughter Ring*. Philadelphia, Jewish Publication Society of America, 1941; *The Merry Heart*. New York, Bookman Associates, 1951.

Millgram, Abraham E., *Sabbath, the Day of Delight*. Philadelphia, Jewish Publication Society of America, 1944.

Neches, Solomon Michael, *Humorous Tales of Latter Day Rabbis*. Los Angeles, Western Jewish Institute, 1945; *As Twas Told to Me*. Los Angeles, 1926.

Newman, Louis I., *The Hasidic Anthology*. New York, Bloch Publishing Co., 1944.

Olsvanger, Immanuel, *L'Chayim!* New York, Schocken Books, 1949; *Royte Pomerantsen*. New York, Schocken Books, 1947.

Persky, Daniel, *Zemanim Tovim*. New York, Pardes, 5704; *Matamim Le-Hag*. New York, Pardes, 1939; *Likhvod Ha-Regel*. New York, 5707; *Tzhok Me-Eretz Yisrael*. New York, 5711.

Ravnitzki, J. H., *Yiddishe Witzen*. New York, Morris S. Sklarsky, 1950. 2 vols.

Richman, Jacob, *Laughs from Jewish Lore*. New York, Funk and Wagnalls Co., 1926; *Jewish Wit and Wisdom*. New York, Pardes Publishing House, 1952.

Schauss, Hayyim, *The Jewish Festivals*. Cincinnati, Union of American Hebrew Congregations, 1938.

Sharfstein, Zvi, *Sefer Ha-Tzhok*. New York, Shiloh, 1930.

Sedan, Dov, *Kaarat Egozim*. Tel Aviv, M. Newman Publishing House, 5713; *Kaarat Tzimukim*. Tel Aviv, M. Newman Publishing House, 5710.

Solis-Cohen, Emily, Jr., *Hanukkah: The Feast of Lights*. Philadelphia, Jewish Publication Society of America, 1937.

Teitelbaum, Elsa, *An Anthology of Jewish Humor and Maxims*. New York, Pardes Publishing House, 1945.

Tendlau, Abraham, *Sprichworter Und Redensarten*. Berlin, Schocken Verlag, 1934.

Unterman, Isaac, *Likvod Yom Tov*. New York, Wolf Sales and Bernard Morgenstern, 1946.

Zlotnick, Isaiah, *Yamim Tovim Folklor*. Warsaw, 1930.